HOW TO

Crazy Amazing®

DURING DIFFICULT TIMES

A compilation of short stories & advice featuring

Irene Abbou

Jesse Brisendine

Dr. Brittany Fernandez

Monica Gonzales

Tami Holzman

John Kralik

Jocelyn Kuhn

Iris Polit

Jairek Robbins

Ann Marie Smith

Jake Sperley

Kyle Tolzman

Whitnie Wiley

Michelle Eades

How to be CRAZY AMAZING® During Difficult Times:
A compilation of short stories & advice

ISBN: 978-1-7350729-1-3 (PB)

Dedication

This book is dedicated to all my fellow humans. You have everything it takes to be Crazy Amazing®. It's my heart's desire that you go out and be Crazy Amazing®. Create the life of your dreams and live to your full potential.

Acknowledgements

I am beyond grateful to my parents, Lupe and Connie Esparza. You taught me how to always look for the positive in every situation. To my Crazy Amazing® husband Matt, you are my biggest cheerleader and make me want to be and do more. My beautiful kids, Kaitlyn and Michael, everyday I want to be my best for you and open doors for you both so that you continue to be Crazy Amazing®. To my sisters Monica, Heather and Yolanda and my brothers John and Joel who inspire me everyday to push harder. To Tina and Jocelyn for putting all of my ideas into motion and seeing the vision and believing it. I love you all!

Contents

Introduction

What are difficult times? I believe that each of us define difficulty based on our own experiences and where we are in life. A child for example, may find sharing their toys with their siblings as difficult. A teen may find communicating with their parents as difficult. An adult who loses their job may find themselves dealing with difficult times. The Oxford dictionary defines difficult as "hard to deal with or get on with".

No matter where you are in life, we all have faced situations that we find are "hard to deal with or hard to get on with". It's in those moments that we feel uncertain about our future. We may be scared, stressed, anxious and maybe hopeless. Let's face it, it is scary to be in a difficult situation.

But why is it that some people thrive during difficult times? What do they do during those times that move them passed the difficulty? Viktor Frankl, in one of my favorite books, Man's Search for Meaning, said something that I have lived by for the last 22 years. He said, *"Everything can be taken from a man but one thing: the last of the human freedoms—to choose one's attitude in any given set of circumstances, to choose one's own way."*

To choose our attitude in any given circumstance, to choose our own way. Think about what that means. A simple shift in our attitude, an opportunity to choose your path. How empowering would that be? Look back at your life, what if those "difficult" times opened up the opportunity for a new life? Maybe a new job? Maybe a new mate? Maybe a greater appreciation for life?

I wish I could tell you that you will never face a difficult time in your life. That you've reached your difficult cap and difficulties are the thing of the past. Sorry, not going to happen. But what I can tell you is that this book is filled with strategies from some of the most Crazy Amazing® people I am blessed to have crossed paths with. They come from all walks of life. All with backgrounds that are diverse. What they share is their ability to not only face difficulties, but to come out of difficult situations on their terms.

These authors not only come out of difficult times, they will share with you what they are doing to be Crazy Amazing® and will inspire you to live a life that is astonishing to an extreme degree. To be such an inspiration to others. To live a life that is filled with positive behaviors that are jaw-dropping to an extreme degree; over the top stunning. These authors will show you how to be Crazy Amazing® during difficult times.

Ann Marie Smith

1

Thank You God for the Pause

— By Ann Marie Smith —

I t was at 3:37 pm on Friday March 13th, 2020 that I received a call that left me with an ache in the pit of my stomach. Our schools were shutting down. One of my companies is an extended learning program that provides after school support for students in grades K-12. This closure of schools also affected my own teenage kids.

I'm not one to panic, but this sudden closure, the news of a virus we knew little about, and the future of my 400 employees left me a little scared. I had a swarm of calls and texts asking me questions that I had no answers to. Now, they were scared, I was numb. I love solving problems, and to my own credit I think I'm pretty good at it, except for the time I rescued 5

Persian cats and adopted them out, only to have to re-rescue 4 of them. So yes, they have their forever home with us, problem solved right?

It's now Monday, March 15th, and we have 'stay-at-home' orders in California. That means we are to stay home. I'm a pretty active person and run several companies with my husband. I wake up every morning and hit the ground running and don't stop until bedtime. In fact, the last time I took an extended leave of absence was to have my children, and even then, I worked from home. I love to work, and I love being busy. But now *this* was going to be my new normal.

I started by organizing our companies. We moved people who could work remotely to work from their homes. Those that had transferable skills went to companies that were labeled "essential". Next, we set up our teens to be able to do online or distance learning. My husband and I work from home, so that was a no-brainer. Next, we made sure that our parents were safe and that we could communicate with them. My father in law lives with us, so that was easy. My active, 80 year old parents were a different story. They love their daily drive to the market and their weekly breakfast at Denny's. It broke my heart to tell them that they were now going to be confined to staying home. I knew that at 80 and 81 years old, they were very vulnerable to getting sick, and that wasn't a risk my brother and sister were willing to take. So, we arranged FaceTime calls, weekly grocery deliveries and drive-bys. I am extremely grateful that 9 weeks into it, they have stayed home and are both healthy and happy.

My life went from the pretty rigid schedule of Monday,

Tuesday, Wednesday, Thursday, Friday, to everyday is today. For the first time in my life I didn't go to bed at any particular time. I didn't have to wake up at any particular time. I realized that I could get by with 2 pairs of clean underwear, 2 pairs of sweats, and 2 pairs of socks. For the first time in my life I was able to pause, and take a temporary stop.

For me, to pause was to take a temporary stop of my routine in life. For someone like me, whose mind is always racing with ideas, or thinking about what I'm going to do next, this pause was foreign. I like being home, so that was not a challenge. But what was I *not* doing? What deadline was I not meeting? What project was I not completing? I realized there was nothing to do, no deadline, no project, no one was waiting for me. This was going to be my new normal, at least for the next few months. How was I going to feed my mind? How was I going to continue to live my purpose? What would feed my soul?

I reflected on what has always brought me joy, even in my darkest hour; adding value to others and being of service. That's what I love to do. That's what I attribute my success to. I once read something that Adam Grant said, "The more I help out, the more successful I become. I measure success in what it has done for the people around me. That is the real accolade." I realized that I needed to add value to those around me. So I garnered the help of my husband, kids and family and searched our community for the most vulnerable who were in need of food and basic home essentials. We quickly identified over 200 people that were home-bound either because of their age or a disability. We partnered with our local food distributor and purchased enough food to provide a weekly delivery of groceries. The look on the faces of the people receiving groceries was priceless. All were so overcome with gratitude that they cried tears of joy. One recipient was so grateful, that he said, "I'm a grown man, 85 years old, and I feel so loved right now."

Buying, sorting and delivering groceries to those in need in our community gave me the opportunity to add value. It also fed my soul. John Bunyan once said, "You have not lived today until you have done something for someone who can never repay you." During this time of pause, my husband and I, our children and our family have been able to 'live' because we did something for someone who can never repay us. Most of the recipients have no clue that the gift was from us, but we like it like that. During this pause, we have learned how to feed our soul: through random acts of kindness.

I realized that in my life I was doing a lot of running. I ran errands, I ran companies, I ran the kids to their events, and I grabbed my husband to run with me. Our days and weekends were spent running from this to that and from here to there. I knew we were running. It was just the way it was with two teenage students who were athletes in High School. We ate on the run and the faster the food the better. It's funny how I didn't realize how much I ran, until I stopped.

I stopped running. I no longer had to run errands, run the kids to school and sports, or eat on the run. I was on pause. I now had lots of time. Every day since March 13th, I've had time to cook. I laugh when I cook something and my kids say, "Mom we had no idea you were such a good cook." Who knew?

My husband and I cook breakfast, lunch, dinner and snacks. I've even taken up baking! I'm not gonna lie, I haven't quite yet mastered baking bread, but my pecan sandies are to die for. Thanks to the pause our family is eating healthy food. We are eating together, laughing and really enjoying each other. I told them a few days ago that I love being quarantined with them and that I am truly going to miss all this time together when the 'stay-at-home' order is lifted.

I was talking to my good friend Michelle about how grateful I was to my God for giving me this pause. She was too cute when she said, "You have spent over 22 years building, with this pause you now have time to enjoy what you have built." Wow! This pause has given me the time to feed my soul by feeding those in need. This pause has given me the time to really enjoy my husband and my kids. This pause has made me realize how much I physically miss my parents, brother, sister and their families. We are going on a long family vacation as soon as we can. This pause has given me the opportunity to feed my family homemade, wholesome food and to eat it together. We have all actually lost some weight. This pause has given me the time to enjoy each of my pets, and yes that includes my 4 rescued cats. This pause has given me the time to really enjoy my home; our family room, our kitchen, our dining table. I didn't realize that we have spent so much time building; building a career, building a family, building for the future. I realized that without this pause, we may have missed out on enjoying it.

We are now 9 weeks into the quarantine. I am beyond grateful to God for this pause. I honor the 'stay-at-home' order as my way of not spreading this virus. I also choose to add value to others. What I have found is that it is possible to be Crazy Amazing™ during difficult times. For me, that means serving others through random acts of kindness. It doesn't have to be big. It's as simple as posting a positive quote on social media. It could be going through your contacts daily and calling one of them to thank them for something they have either said or done for you. For me it also means giving my family my best effort and cooking and baking for them. It also means being present for them.

It was 3:37 pm on March 13th. The day that changed my life. The day I learned to pause. I thank God for the opportunity to pause and to learn that there's a time for building and a time for pausing. May you all take this time to enjoy the pause.

2

A Simple Act of Gratitude

— By John Kralik —

A virus has brought a cruel season to the world, and it has remained through winter, spring and summer. As we seek to survive this season, examples of meanness abound, and it is easy to curse the darkness. Yet each of us can light a small spark of kindness, kindle a small bit of goodness around us.

For me, gratitude has always marked the beginning of the way back from anger. This has been true in my personal life. Even those people with whom I have a difficult relationship have had their hearts opened up when I wrote them thank-you notes. And when I write thank-you notes, my heart opens too.

Although short like a tweet, a thank you note is an

anti-tweet: there is only enough room to be thankful, and to express a bit of love. The goal is to find and focus on a single good thing that someone has done. There will be time later for all the rest. It is a simple act, with only one goal: to express love. Today, I feel as though I am the living proof that it can change your life.

I have tried to continue the journey of writing one note per day since the beginning of this season. For fifteen days, I shared on Facebook the background of the note I was writing. These are the notes I shared during those fifteen days.

Day 1—Grateful for my Journey

My book, and my initial journey began during the 2008 financial crisis. It was a struggle then to find something to be grateful for each day. But I did, and as I came out of that time I realized I had blessings beyond what I could have hoped for, and grace I didn't know existed. Two months ago, I was called by difficulties in my own life, to return to my journey of writing one thank-you note a day. Little did I know how much I would need that regimen, and how it would provide a little place of order and continuity in a time of confusion and chaos.

It has been so long since I've even looked at Facebook, feeling that it has become a flashpoint of division rather than a gathering place of love and strength. I am looking at Facebook today only because it is the only way I can attend the Church that I found in my gratitude journey. My thank you note today will be to our Pastor, Dave Roberts, for continuing to minister to us in a way that directly addresses the role that each of us must play now that our usual roles have been taken away. I have decided that sharing a little about gratitude will be one role I can play.

As I am a person who is blessed beyond measure, I know it will be easy for me to find something to be grateful for each day in the midst of a situation that is dire for so many.

Day 2—Grateful for Health Care Workers

Today is Doctor's Day. And so it is necessary and right for today's thank you note to be addressed to my primary care physician Dr. Marina Manvelyan. She practices in Pasadena, California. Dr. Manvelyan has seen me through four immune system-related hospitalizations in the last four years. She has helped me reach a plateau where I feel strong and ready should this latest scourge come my way. I am often grateful to her for all she has done for me in the last 30 years; she has righted my path numerous times and kept me here to enjoy the many benefits of my life.

There are many doctors, nurses and physicians' assistants to thank this month. Those who clean the hospitals have become central players. We are just understanding how crucial they are, how important their jobs are.

As we are all in this lockdown now, I hope you will join me in the renewal of my thank you note journey. I have been blessed and privileged by my journey, so I am in a much better place than many, and certainly in a much better place than in

2008 when I wrote my book, *A Simple Act of Gratitude*. Please inspire yourself by writing a thank you note to a health care worker today.

Day 3—Grateful for People in Service Professions

Many of us will be in isolation for at least 30 more days. Today's thank you note was to the woman who cleans our house. We are not only blessed to have someone help with our cleaning, but also because we are able to tell her not to come for a while. We could pay her to stay home with her family today. We are blessed by what her hard work has brought to our family. And hard work it is! I tried doing some of it myself today. One of my biggest issues is that I'm still about a month away from noticing that the house isn't that clean. Nevertheless, I was vacuuming away.

If you are lucky enough to have someone cleaning your house, give them the day off. If you are lucky enough to be able to pay them anyway, go ahead and do it. And write a thank you note to them.

Day 4—Gratitude for Essential Workers

One of the hardest things for me to accept during this crisis is that I am 'non-essential'. I have been working continuously since I became a camp counselor after my junior year of high school. Since then, I have always had a part-time or full-time job, and never more than 2 weeks' vacation at a time. Now, as a member of a risk group, I am supposed to stay home and do nothing.

For today's thank you note, I am writing to a group of essential people. Last night, we ordered a pizza from La Canada Imports, which is where we always order from. It showed up hot and on-time and was exactly as it always was. As we sat and ate that pizza, everything seemed alright again. As I have often explained to my personal trainer, every American has a constitutional right to one pizza per week. Pizza is essential.

So if you have time today, write a note to the essential people who are still cooking and delivering your pizza. As for me, I need to accept that my role is to flatten the curve by staying home and avoiding, as best I can, the need to be in a hospital anytime soon. I am greatly blessed that I have succeeded in this passive role so far.

Day 5—More Gratitude for Essential Workers

Today my gratitude is still focused on essential workers, those working away on our street. Last night we weren't motivated to cook—again—so relied on a staple take out of hamburgers and fries from Everest Burgers. Too many things are different now. I found myself especially thankful for the things that remain the same.

I ate the fries on the way home, as always, as we once did

when we were kids and McDonald's was the most amazing thing in our lives.

I mentioned the constitutional amendment that allows every American to eat one pizza per week. It has a second clause that refers to hamburgers and fries. So if you can, thank your local hamburger stand. Keep them in business and if possible, let them keep the change. Why not? It's probably a fearful urban legend—so many of them abound—that the change from your dollar can transfer the disease, but generosity can provide the remedy.

Day 6—And More Gratitude for Essential Workers

We ventured to the grocery store this morning. My thank you note was addressed to the essential workers at our local Ralph's at 2675 Foothill Blvd. The store was clean and well stocked. The crowds were gone. At last there were eggs.

As shoppers we must all look both frightened and frightening (now with the masks for heaven's sake). Yet everyone was working away, so professionally, as if it was an ordinary day. I was thankful to be able to get flowers and fresh food.

If you have a chance to thank your local grocery workers, with a note or a flower or otherwise, please take it today. When I went to use the treadmill in the garage, my wife asked what we should do with the chicken. "How about fried chicken?", I suggested. When I came back in, the smell of fried chicken filled the house. I am blessed and full to the brim, thanks to her.

Day 7—Gratitude for Those Who are Sharing the Journey

For many out there, quarantine or "sheltering in place," has been a sentence to solitary confinement. However, I am blessed to have my companion and love in quarantine with me: my wife Catherine. So today's thank you note is to her. She has been patient with my impatience. She has not been irritated at the little irritating things that I do even though she now has to endure them all day long. She has been positive when it has been so easy to be negative. She has decided to have good days when the situation dictated otherwise. She has focused on my health and well-being, when I have lost that focus. Her love has been evident at every turn.

If you are lucky enough to have someone with you during this difficult time, and if they are doing their best to make it better, try writing them a thank you note and telling them why you are grateful. Today.

Day 8—Gratitude for Voices Not Our Own

There are so many voices and more ways than ever for these voices to insist on being heard, even when we would rather shut them out. Recent years have taught us to both question and fear the underlying agendas of those who present us with facts. Even numbers sometimes especially numbers, can be misleading, something this crisis has shown us several times.

In times like these, it is important to find a way to exchange ideas with those we truly trust and know to have good judgment. They provide us a safe sounding board on which to test our own impressions and gain greater understanding of what we should and shouldn't believe. I am especially grateful for these voices, and the wisdom that they bring to me each day. Yesterday's thank you was to my wife, someone whom I can rely on to balance me. When you are alone with yourself, it is so easy to start talking nonsense. There are a few other voices I have come to rely on as well.

The social distancing requirements and bans on meetings have severely affected Alcoholics Anonymous and other 12-Step Programs which rely on the in-person support of the group meetings. They are soldiering on, meeting outside in parks, using the video communication website 'Zoom', which I learned how to use today.

Several years ago, I was privileged enough to speak at a church in Akron, Ohio. After the service, I made a pilgrimage to Dr. Bob's House, the home of one of the founders of Alcoholics Anonymous. I picked up a card there, which I found while cleaning out a file today. It tells a story Dr. Bob often told, about how camels kneel at the beginning of each day to take up their burden, and then again at the end of the day to lay it down. In the same way, Dr. Bob would say, God gives us only what we can carry each day.

I'm using this card today to send a thank you note to someone I know who is continuing to provide support and wisdom to those in Alcoholics Anonymous, even during this time of crisis. If you know of someone who is continuing to support a

12-Step Program during this difficult time, thank them today. They are essential.

We are one day closer, one day at a time. May God give you only what you can carry.

Day 9—More Gratitude for Voices Not Our Own

I am not yet running out of things for which to be grateful. I continue to be grateful for those who I can talk to, whose voices I know and trust.

During my initial journey of gratitude, I renewed my friendship with my college roommate. This past fall, we returned to Michigan to go to a football game and visit my daughter, who is now a sophomore. We were staying in a Red Roof Inn, but we might as well have been back in the dorm. From the moment we met at the airport to the moment we said goodbye in the concourse, we didn't stop talking.

Over the last few weeks, we have been talking and emailing, trying to make sense of it all. Relationships from college or high school can be so valuable because in those days, you just made friends for friendship's sake. There was no need to look at people as prospective clients, bosses or subordinates, allies or adversaries. Nowadays, I have to look at everyone in Los Angeles as a potential lawyer, litigant or juror.

Yesterday, we both needed to learn how to use 'Zoom' for our upcoming meetings, so we worked together over the phone to figure it out. We set up a meeting and met on Zoom to discuss the state of the world. Obviously we didn't fix anything, but we understood it a little better.

So today's thank you note is to my old roommate. As we went through the numbers, we encountered the slightest turning point, the beginning of a hope for the end. So if you have an old friend who is helping you to understand this crisis better, say thank you to them today.

I am grateful today that we are one day closer to the end. I long to return to Michigan with my old friend.

Day 10: Grateful for the Voices behind the Masks.

I am thankful for a smile and a 'hello', even if it's through a mask or from across the street. I went for a walk today, maintaining social distance, of course. Sometimes, I had to cross the street or walk out into the road, which was astonishingly devoid of cars.

In some moments I worry that COVID-19 will change everything. Just as the internet changed everything, only worse. Today it felt like some of the people who passed me were skittering away, worried that I carried the plague like a zombie in 'The Walking Dead.' But many seemed to recognize how necessary a smile or a wave is these days. A simple hello or "how're you doing?" can warm the worry for a moment and remind us that one day we will gather together again.

So for today my thank you is an electronic shout out to those who smiled or waved or said hello—even if they were scared I was a possible asymptomatic carrier. You made my day and bore the cheer on the sad day that John Prine's eloquent voice left us. We needed him to sing tonight of the 'illegal smile' that my fellow walkers shared with me today. It don't cost very much, but it lasts a long while. God rest you John, and I pray you may sing with Steve Goodman again.

Day 11—Grateful that the Trash is Still Picked Up

On my walk today I saw the truck picking up the trash. As I did, I shared a wave and a smile with the driver. It was a relief and brought me great comfort to see him working, doing his essential job. His truck was one of the few vehicles I encountered. With all of us staying at home, with all this fervent cleaning of every microbe, with all the hauling in of supplies, the garbage is undoubtedly piling up significantly more than usual. Where would we be if all the wipes and paper towels, the single use plastic take out boxes, disposable gloves and masks were not being carted away? We would all be wallowing in the things we are trying so desperately to avoid and wash away.

Taking the trash cans in and out gave me something to do, and I was grateful for that too. The rain had washed them down the hill. L.A. has been awash in rain. It feels as though it's been raining since this all started. I don't think I've ever seen the city cleaner. You can see the stars at night, and when the skies clear of rain, you can see out to the ocean from the San Gabriel Mountains. I wish the trails were open so we feel their comfort again, but even on the street the smell of fuel has dissipated and you can breathe in and smell the new growth of trees and flowers all around. I'm sorry to say so, but as wonderful as it all is, I would trade it all to go back to work. I'm trying to complete a novel about someone who hates his job, but, suddenly, I think I would love just about any job. So long as I was allowed to actually do it.

I had no idea what company was taking out the trash, but I did the research necessary to write a thank you note to the fellow in that truck. I hope the company gets it to him. While I was doing the research, I found out I might be entitled to a senior discount when I turn 65 in a week or two. This was my silver lining of the day.

If your trash got picked up today, try thanking the workers who made that possible. They are essential now and always.

The curve is flattening, they say, but every data point on the curve is a real human being. No one ever adds that flattening the curve will lengthen the curve, prolonging the cruel season to no object. No one admits that in the end, the number lost will be about the same no matter what we do.

Today was the worst of days for those families who have lost a loved one to the disease, or just because their time had come. My prayers are with them tonight.

Day 12—Grateful for the Mail

On Monday, we received no mail. Not a bill, a credit card

application, or even a political solicitation. Not even an invitation to join the AARP (we did get that today though).

Nevertheless, the mail remains essential and it's getting more so. It's one of our few remaining lifelines to the outside world. At the invitation of my pharmacy, I've been getting my prescriptions by mail, and that is a good thing.

The downturn in mail is apparently happening everywhere, which is causing financial problems for the Postal Service. The same publication that brought that financial news today also had a feature about how much better it is to write a letter than an email. Perhaps there is something we can do there!

Today's thank you is to our mail carrier. I don't know how exactly, but I will get it to him or her. Lately I've been noticing the mail trucks more, as they are a predominant part of the remaining traffic on the road. With this in mind, I think I can accomplish getting this thank you letter to the mail carrier. I promise to keep a proper social distance. Unfortunately, I'm embarrassed to say that I don't know the brave person who has been faithfully doing their job every day as they usually come after I've left for mine.

Nonetheless, I will make it happen.

So thank your mail carrier when you see them, and keep them in business by sending thank you notes and letters to those you love.

Day 13—Grateful for a Mother's Smile

The information seemed so confusing today. Facts must be

distinguished from things we have been told because the powers that be people want us to believe them for our own good, as it is variously perceived. Rather than agonize over the things I cannot change, I searched for something for which to be grateful.

Walking through cold and rainy Los Angeles today, I received a Facetime from my mother, who is 94. She seemed quite impressed that my phone was waterproof, and that I could stop and talk to her in the rain.

I was most grateful to see her smile, and so I wrote to thank her for that. "When you smile and laugh, you bring joy to our hearts" I wrote. Are you thankful for someone's smile today? If so, let them know.

Day 14—Gratitude for Work

Thanks to my research attorney, I needed to actually *do* something similar to what I would normally define as my work. As I needed my work computer to review the files for the five cases she had completed, I made my normal pilgrimage into the office—in half the time. There is a thrill to driving in L.A. without the traffic and a sense of longing that it could always be so.

When I got to work, I was the only one in the building, so there was no problem observing the posted policies on social distancing. But of course, my computer set-up no longer functioned, and the able fellow who normally sorts through the spaghetti wires was not there to help me. My own limited skills failed me. Nevertheless, the process of going to work gave my day a sense of structure and purpose for which I was grateful. I left thank you notes for my research attorney, my clerk and courtroom assistant, all of whom have come in at various times to keep things from falling apart, instead of just grinding to a standstill.

When I returned home, I was grateful there was even more to do. I was able to assist my wife in cleaning out the gutters after all the rain, washed my car, and attended to other things to keep myself feeling useful. After a session on the treadmill, I actually felt tired, and hungry. My wife made some incredibly good chili, after which I felt I had also earned some chocolate ice cream.

After dinner, I was sorting through some of the papers my father left behind when he died last year. Among the papers he left on his desk, I found a motivational pamphlet from the 1950's. He had underlined the following statement: "I've learned that I have to work in order to be happy. People need work almost as badly as they need food; without it they're devoured by restlessness and discontent." So true then. So true now.

I was grateful for the first thank you note I received regarding the book's inspiration during the current crisis. The note itself was on some "Keep Calm and Carry On" stationery. I'm guessing I'm not the only one searching for a sense of gratitude in this time. If someone gave your life a sense of purpose today by giving you something to do that felt like work, consider writing them a thank you.

Day 15—Grateful for Easter and Easter Services

For Easter, we were invited to a truly special private backyard service put together by my friend Rob for his wife Jeannette and four friends, of which we were two. Rob was concerned that there be two or more gathered together today. With tremendous thought and energy, he made it happen, while still giving due respect for all applicable laws. There were flowers, and a beautiful program he had designed. He gave each of us a role in reading a part of the Easter Story from Matthew, Mark, Luke and John, which was woven together to make it complete. Flowers were set amid chairs arranged at a perfect social distance. Masks were indeed reluctantly worn in consideration of the immune problems of some attendees, including, I suppose, me. A simple tune was sung, one that we could all carry. We sang of God's 'Amazing Grace'.

This will be my final, publicly mentioned thank you note of this brief journey back onto the pages of Facebook. I got up each morning not knowing what I would write about or who I would address it to. I found myself wondering if I could find something for which to be grateful each day of a pandemic. I thought if I could show that it is possible for me to be grateful, then others would seek to do so as well. I hope and pray that has happened, and that I have demonstrated the continuing possibility of this type of journey. For it is during these dark times, that it is most necessary.

Of course, my thank you note journey will continue in

private. I have reached 1600 thank yous, with a goal of writing thousands more.

I recognize that this exercise has become so easy for me because I am fortunate enough to have been unscathed by the current events. It is my fond hope that this brief exercise will assist those who have journeys behind and before them much more difficult than my own. Facebook is a tool that can be used for good or evil, and there is a fine line between what is inspiring and helpful and what is annoying and repetitive. It is my hope that I have stopped before crossing that line for you.

Carry On. Love is coming. Someday soon, I pray.

3

COVID-19 Self Isolation: An Early Birthday Gift

— By Jairek Robbins —

When the novel Coronavirus was first detected in China at the end of 2019, hardly anyone in the U.S. gave serious thought to it. Before long however, COVID-19 was detected on U.S. soil and a cascade of stay at home orders were issued across the nation as people scrambled to understand what was going on.

You may be wondering why I have referred to this self-isolation (or lockdown) as an early birthday present instead of a forced time of suffering. I call it a gift or an opportunity because it gives each one of us a unique chance to reveal the leader in us. We are all leaders in our own right, and there is no better time to prove this than now.

In my best-selling book 'LIVE IT! Achieve Success by Living with Purpose' I focus on the idea that we should be a living testament of the message we are sending out into the world. The ongoing lockdown is a gift because it has allowed us to build ourselves, our relationships, and to help others in several ways during this turbulent time.

1. Building Ourselves into the Best Version We Can Be

You cannot give what you do not have, and the task of inspiring and giving hope to others starts with putting in the work each day in order to become an example of what's possible. During this time, we have been engaging in a number of activities to build the happiest, strongest, healthiest and most fulfilled versions of ourselves. These include;

- Starting the day with an ice-cold shower that lasts at least 3 minutes. This helps to reset the body physically, emotionally and also boosts the immune system.
- 20 minutes of breathing exercises in the morning and evening is key to resetting your body's nervous system to calm. It involves breathing in to a count of 4 seconds and then breathing out to a count of 8 seconds. The app 'Breathe' has been very helpful as a guide to maintain this breath pattern for 20 min each session.
- Stretching or yoga exercises to keep the body flexible. A flexible mind and body is key in chaotic times.

- 30 minutes of exercise to access the endorphins that come from an elevated heart rate. This helps us feel strong and confident in who we are.
- 10 minutes of meditation each day. The site www.highperformancemuse.com is helpful for this.
- A walk in nature each morning. During this walk, my wife and I do an exercise in which we share three things that we are grateful for about each other. This routine helps to strengthen our connection as it reminds us of how important we are to each other.
- Future vision planning. During our daily walk, we also discuss what kind of vision we can build for our future together. This keeps us firmly focused on building a life *together* instead of growing apart. We ensure that while each person pursues their own vision, we too have a joint vision as a couple.
- Having healthy and wholesome meals every day. This is crucial because you are what you eat!

Scientific proof suggests that these actions are in fact associated with an increase in both overall happiness and success in one's career, relationships, business, health, creativity, community involvement, job, and so many other spheres of human endeavor.

2. Building a Deeper Relationship With Each Other

Most of what I shared earlier is primarily aimed at building an individual to develop into the best version of themselves.

However, some of the activities, such as taking nature walks in the morning, sharing what we are grateful for about each other and discussing our future vision, work to build a strong bond between us as a couple.

In addition to those activities, we have done more to build a deeper relationship with each other. For example, my wife undertook a program called "In Sync with the Opposite Sex." This program, offered by www.understandingmen.com has been so useful in helping her understand how a man thinks and looks at the world, which has prevented a lot of avoidable friction between us.

Myself, I signed up for the Level 1 & 2 certification program at www.gottman.com on how to improve our marriage. These people have been studying more than 3000 couples over a period of 30 years and have reported their scientific findings on what makes relationships work and how one can increase their chance of being happy in their marriage for decades to come. You've probably heard how the lockdowns have strained relationships, so now may be the best time to enroll for this program.

One of the most useful tools shared in that program that anyone can immediately put to use in their relationship, is the tool of using the right words when communicating with a partner about emotions, specific events or one's needs.

When communicating one shoud use the following three prompts:

I feel… (specific emotion)

When… (specific situation)

I need…. (specific need or support)

The Gottman Institute also recommends that when listening to your partner, one should use these three steps:

Step 1: Mirror back what you heard.

Step 2: Validate how that must make them feel

Step 3: Empathize and share how you would feel if that was happening to you.

For example, you can mirror by repeating phrases mentioned by your partner in order to show them that you are listening attentively to what they are saying. This can make your partner feel valued, and subsequently your relationship will likely strengthen.

During this pandemic, we are using every opportunity we get to implement what we learned from these programs and the journey has been an exciting one!

3. Helping Small Businesses Navigate This Chaotic Time

The third area we have been focusing on during this chaotic time is helping small business owners weather the storm and keep their business alive. Our goal is to help them survive the storm and then to help them thrive as the economy and world begins to open back up. We use these simple three 'P' steps to help them do this.

- **Protect.** We encourage small business owners to take

a close look at their businesses and identify the aspects of that business that are healthy. Once these are identified, steps must be taken to protect those healthy components so that they aren't negatively impacted during this pandemic.

- **Pivot.** We also urge small business owners to identify the aspects of their businesses that aren't doing so well. The purpose here is to see how those aspects can be pivoted so that they don't become the dead weight which brings down the entire business amid this ongoing chaos.

- **Profit.** The third 'P' offers small businesses a chance to look for a new opportunity that can propel the business to grow new income streams amid the chaos. Times of crisis can be disruptive in a very bad way, but when the correct lenses are used to look at the situation, unforeseen opportunities present themselves. For instance, who knew that it would become normal to talk to your doctor via Zoom and get a prescription? The ongoing chaos has changed the rules, created new needs and burst peoples' bubbles of comfort. We encourage small businesses to look closely and find an opportunity they can act on and propel their businesses to new levels of profitability!

A simple thing you can do if you are a small business owner is this straightforward exercise. Let's start with identifying the oxygen upon which your business depends. Humans are able to survive without food for up to 30 days, without water for 3-5 days, and without oxygen for only 3-5 minutes. Similarly, businesses need oxygen called "operating cash." This shouldn't be mistaken for profits, rather, it is the cash that the business needs to address its ongoing expenses.

To protect this oxygen, we ask business owners to categorize every expense as either being green, yellow or red. All expenses that are absolutely necessary are categorized as **GREEN**. For expenses that they could do without but are needed by the business to some extent, a **YELLOW** categorization is given. Any expenses that you are incurring but don't need at all, fall into the **RED** category. I call these the 'WTH expenses', which may include subscriptions to industry journals that you never get around to reading or buying social media followers. Cut these out immediately!

Over the past few weeks we have done this simple exercise with business owners around the globe and are thrilled to share that they have been able to save between $3000 - $300,000 off of their 2020 expenses.

This brings me back to where I started. To me, this pandemic has given me an early birthday present (it is my birthday month currently) because it has allowed me to add more fuel to my efforts to grow as a person, to enrich my relationship with my wife, and to help small businesses take a cold, hard look at the way they work. In doing so they are able to shed excess fat and capitalize on any opportunities available. My belief is that if these lessons become a routine part of how we live our lives, then society will have benefited greatly from this pandemic. See you on the other side!

For those of you that have lost loved ones in this chaotic

time: a friend once told me that life is like the mist, once it soaks into you it will be part of you forever. Any time you want to connect with a loved one, just close your eyes and imagine having a deep and loving conversation with them in your mind. It is a simple, powerful way to reconnect with the most beautiful parts of them.

4

How Are You, Really?

— By Tami Holzman —

Someone I once dated called me recently, and my heart skipped a beat. In my Ex's voice mail message, the Ex said he had a question and decided to call instead of text (hmmm). My neurotic mind started to race! Why did my heart skip a beat? What did my reaction mean? Did I still have feelings for him? Did he have feelings for me? Or was I having an unpredictable response because I'm not sure what happened to us in the first place? Was there ever really an "us?" Was I crazy? Am I crazy?

Lucky for you, I will save my unresolved love-life issues for another book!

In the meantime, I called him back and left a VM. The

past couple of months had felt like we were living an episode of the Twilight Zone (it's April 24, 2020, and the world is in the middle of a global pandemic, should anyone be reading this in 2055). I told him it was great to hear his voice, and I came clean about my heart skipping a beat. I mean, why not? We may all die anyway.

The Ex and I finally connected the next day (which felt like two years). As we got caught up, chit-chatting about our families -- he paused -- then asked how I was doing. I had an unexpected reaction. I started to cry. It was a bit embarrassing, but then again, screw it. I am working on being more vulnerable in my love life anyway!

In addition to the global health crisis, I had serious stuff going on. Aside from the loss of income from Covid19 related restrictions, a girl I've sponsored for 11 years in Cambodia ran away from home (now possibly homeless and alone). My dad had just been released from the hospital with some random life-threatening disease. All the stress and worry caused my autoimmune disorder, scleroderma, to kick in, which left me covered in non-human like hives and my confidence at an all-time low.

You may ask: who cares about an ex-boyfriend calling out of the blue and asking how I was doing?

And I would agree, but an important detail to add to the equation is what he said precisely, "I WAS THINKING ABOUT YOU and everything you have going on, and wanted to know how you are doing?"

It seems like a simple story, and quite frankly (besides my unresolved issues with the man), it is! And, that is the point.

If you think about it, asking someone how they're REALLY doing can change one's whole perspective – be it that day, that week, or the rest of their life. That is how great an impact EMPATHY has on us; empathy is everyone's non-judgemental best friend, favorite blanket, and best companion.

When I was asked to contribute to this book, I thought: What am I doing for the world that is so special? Probably nothing too earth-shattering. Except, I care too about how other people are feeling – really! I coach business leaders and executives on the importance of being empathetic, but I also practice empathy every day. For me, it comes naturally. I show up, and it may not be perfect, I may flounder, however, you can count on me to be there.

Empathy is not exclusive to our personal lives; it belongs in business too. We spend 90k hours of our life at work, a 10:1 ratio of who we spend time with otherwise. We need to feel empathy toward our peers. You can't go wrong if you lead with your heart.

Harvard Business Review recently published an article by Karyn Twaronite aptly titled, "The Surprising Power of Simply Asking Coworkers How They're Doing." In it, she says:

"As humans, we have an innate need to belong – to one another, our friends, families, culture, and country. The same is true when we're at work. When people feel like they belong at work, they are more productive, motivated, and engaged, and

3.5 times more likely to contribute to their fullest potential according to our research at the Center for Talent Innovation."

At some point, we are all going to experience the death of a loved one, a break-up, a job loss, discrimination, a health crisis, a natural disaster, or even a global pandemic (who would have thought?). No matter the circumstance, these things are tough, scary, and lonely. However, once we are present with our empathy and take down our walls, we can indeed be there for one another. Essentially, there will be no mistakes in what we say or how we say it as long as we show up with our whole heart.

Here are five empathy tips for building your empathy skills (just in case)!

1. Saying something. We have all witnessed, if not experienced, firsthand when a hard topic can be avoided because people are afraid of saying the wrong thing. Something is better than nothing, but remember to connect to the feeling underpinning the issue.

It can be as simple as:
- "How are you doing, really?"
- "I don't know what to say, but know that I love you (We don't need to know what to say).
- "If and when you want to talk, I am here for you!"

2. Listen with an open heart. Just as important as not being silent, is the ability to listen to others. We don't need to have all the answers, even if we have experienced a similar loss. You must become the listener, not the knower. We don't all process feelings the same way. For example, if you've already lost your father and a friend loses theirs, the loss is not parallel. (Maybe yours was a loving father, and your friend had an absent father). Most of the time, the point is that sad or stressed people aren't looking for an answer; they want to be heard and given the opportunity to vent.

You can:
- Be the shoulder they can lean on;
- Be 100% present;
- Try your best not to interrupt, or project your history onto them;
- And, remember these are their feelings, not yours.

3. Be intentionally helpful. Some people don't necessarily know how to respond when offered help directly. Have you ever noticed when you ask someone who seems to be in trouble if they need anything, they say no? It's most likely because they don't want to trouble you.

To combat this:
- It's as easy as checking in on your friend, even a simple text;
- Cook for them or bring them groceries (Often, when we are sad or in crisis, it's crazy how paralyzed we feel);
- And, it never hurts to bring over a bottle of wine, be present, and listen (It's more fun too).

4. Be consistent and reliable. When people are struggling, we tend to send flowers or gifts, and yes, flowers will cheer anyone up. But we need to be mindful and continue to reach out after something happens, once the flower deliveries and phone calls stop. Support and the continued connection is crucial to help maintain one's resilience.

Some ideas are:

- Consider sending a card in the weeks that follow, as a reminder you're there;
- Send them photos of fond memories;
- And, invite a struggling friend for dinner or a video date. Even just the invitation reminds someone they are loved.

5. Heal with laughter. The ability to laugh is the key to sanity and survival. The great Austrian psychiatrist and Holocaust survivor Viktor Frankl attest to as much in his psychological memoir, *Man's Search for Meaning.* And author Madeleine L'Engle said, "A good laugh heals a lot of hurts." There is always humor in the dark, and often, there is healing in laughter. Why do you think it is so cathartic to tell funny stories about the deceased at their funeral?

Try:

- Telling a joke, when the time is right, and it will be;
- Laughing at yourself by sharing an embarrassing story that happened to you;
- Or watch a comedy show or a funny movie.

Speaking of movies, *Sex and the City* is a good reminder of how important it is to be present for someone when they are suffering, and although you may be in a dark time now, you will laugh again. Remember when Carrie was left at the altar by Big? She was humiliated and heartbroken. Kicking and screaming, she ended up going on her honeymoon in Mexico with her best friends but didn't get out of bed for days. When she finally did get out of bed, she asked her friends if she was ever going to laugh again. Samantha said, of course, she would, when something is really, really funny.

Meanwhile, Charlotte was too scared to eat the food in Mexico, for fear of getting Montezuma's revenge. She brought cases of pudding and stayed away from the delicious five-star spread at the hotel. Once Charlotte got comfortable, she began to let her guard down and accidentally drank some water during a shower as it streamed down her face. Moments later, her stomach started to grumble, and she raced back to the room, trying not to shit her pants. En route, Charlotte ran into the girls having drinks. "Sweetie, what's wrong?" they asked. With sweat and humiliation all over her face, she shit her pants. They all laughed so hard they peed their pants! Besides *Sex and the City* being a funny, emotional, and feel-good movie, the film shows that no matter what pain we suffer, we will have better times ahead.

I leave you with this quote:

"I've learned that people will forget what you said, people will forget what you did, but people will never forget how you made them feel."

– Maya Angelou

xo,
Tami Holzman

PS. Since writing this chapter during Covid-19, social activist, and iconic fashion designer Kenneth Cole announced the launch of the "How Are You, Really?" Challenge with The Mental Health Coalition (MHC), the first collaborative effort at a scale which convenes and unites the leading US mental health organizations, creative and media platforms, passionate advocates, politicians, thought leaders, athletes, and celebrities working collectively to de-stigmatize mental health conditions and address the pervasive public health crisis. The Coalition launched with an online platform, a digital resource guide, www.thementalhealthcoalition.org, and an interactive story-telling platform www.howareyoureally.org. The challenge has prompted participation from New York Governor Andrew Cuomo, Whoopi Goldberg, Deepak Chopra, Kesha, Kendall Jenner, Justin and Hailey Bieber, and more.

I can add psychic powers to the list of my superpowers!

5

A Handful of Hope

— By Jesse Brisendine —

My Dear Friend,

I believe you and I are similar. I believe when this all began, we both felt obliged to support others while simultaneously struggling with our own feelings of fear and uncertainty.

My greatest hope is that in sharing my story, it inspires you in living out the next chapter of yours. With that in mind I promise you that I will be transparent, honest, and share from the heart.

Full Transparency:

I am NOT someone who has it all figured out.

I'd be lying if I told you I've thrived through this entire period and greeted every moment of every day with joy and optimism.

I've had my moments; moments filled with fear, self-doubt, and not so silent tears.

I do not own a home, yet.

I am still making payments on my car, for now.

My business had a rough three years (a byproduct of listening to so many self-proclaimed gurus and not enough to my own heart), during which I've borrowed and taken on debt to keep it going. I'm not proud of the debt, but I am proud of the belief behind it – the belief that I know the work I do is why I am here. It's my mission, my purpose and my greatest joy. It's sacred.

My family relationships are ok at best. My brother and I do not communicate. Months, sometimes even years can pass without much more than a "Happy Birthday I love you," text to extended family. However, one bright spot is the relationship I have with my mom, which has grown over the last several years. The biggest reason for this growth has been my decision to love her for who she is and where she is rather than how I wanted her to be.

My friendships are really great. The friends in my life are some of the most sacred and treasured parts of my life.

My health is pretty good. I work out regularly and eat well. I do have a chronic spinal condition that, if I do not take care of every day, will act up and leave me in pain leaning sideways (think of the 'Bent Neck Lady' from 'The Haunting of Hill House').

I've lost a lot of loved ones over the last few years;

One of my best friends to suicide (a self-inflicted gunshot wound to the head – I found him while he was still alive).

My dad a few months after that, who, just two weeks before his death, had been promised more time by his doctor after winning a lengthy battle with cancer.

My best friend was killed in a car accident a couple year later.

Since then, there have been frequent bouts of loss in my life as I lost eight loved ones over a 10-month period. Most recently we had to put my cat down last June. I still cry because I miss her. She is one of my soul mates.

So why, in a book called "Crazy Amazing" did I just spend the first 400 of my allotted words telling you about the less than crazy amazing parts of life? I want to be authentic with you. I want to share with you not as another expert, but as a fellow human being.

This period of time is a very human time. It has caused changes we are all feeling in one way or another.

I, like you, am a human being who has struggled, suffered, and endured challenges. I've felt what you've felt. In some cases, I've even been where you have been (or maybe are right now).

Despite the hardships, when I look back, my life really has been crazy amazing and that is only going to continue. In fact, these last couple months during the COVID-19 pandemic, have honestly been some of the most crazy amazing months of my life.

Why?

One word: Decisions.

The quality of all our lives is determined by the quality of our decisions. Every day we are making 100s of decisions that encompass everything from: how we spend our time, who we love, what we believe about ourselves, and what *this* means. The decisions we make or do not make (I'd argue that indecision is a decision) determine our destiny.

In California where I live, the 'shelter in place' order went into effect on March 19th. Approximately six weeks later (April 29th, 2020), at the time of this writing, the order is still in place, with no definitive date on when it will be rescinded.

During the early moments of what has become the 'new normal', I began to feel the familiar fingers of fear and uncertainty creeping up my spine. You can always feel their presence – whether it's the increased weight of the world or the heaviness you feel in your heart, both are indicators of their unwelcomed presence.

Here's the thing with fear – it's a decision maker too. If you do not make a decision, fear will decide for you.

Consider some of the people you may know who are not living their dreams. If you have a conversation with them, and dig deep enough, you will always find that at the critical moment of decision… the moment they were standing at the crossroads of life and had to decide to travel in a new direction towards their dream, or remain on the same path, fear made the decision for them.

In fact, I'd argue that more often than not, when it comes right down to it, the biggest difference between people who are living crazy amazing lives and those who are not, are the decisions that they chose to make. The ones who are living crazy amazing lives have made definite decisions themselves, whereas everyone else has allowed fear to decide their fate for them.

Recognizing I needed to decide before fear determined my destiny, I grabbed a yellow pad (the same one I wrote the first draft of this on) and scribbled out the following:

Decisions I need to make:

1. Who do I want to be/become during the pandemic?
2. How will I show up to serve/support people?
3. What do I need to do to make that happen? What does the next level of serving/supporting look like?
4. Why is this important?

These are the answers I came up with:

Who: I will be a leader and a magic maker. I will lead from a place of love. I will be a source of empowerment, strength, courage, and hope.

How: Additional support for clients as needed. Can I interview experts to get them to share their best tools, tips, and tactics? Will they be open to this?

What: To see if there is interest for the interviews, I can write a heartfelt Facebook post and ask? I can also email friends/colleges who would be a great fit for this.

Why is this important: I believe humanity, if given the right tools, love and support can emerge from this time happy, healthy, full of love and capable of living deeply fulfilling lives by building thriving businesses (careers) that they are passionate about.

I was terrified of asking if there was an interest in the

interviews. When it comes to conducting interviews, I have zero experience aside from helping my friend Johnny chronicle the last two years of his life to raise awareness about ALS.

Fear began to crawl up my spine and make a beeline for my head and heart. "What if people say no?" "What if no one responds?" "Will I look like a failure?" "If I am interviewing and not "the expert" will that discredit me professionally?" "Can my fragile ego handle that?"

Isn't it funny how, when we get ready to make a decision that we know is the right one, fear manages to take root in your head and attempts to manipulate you into believing even the most unlikely of scenarios? I say unlikely because when we know a truth in our heart, it makes the lies of fear a lot easier to spot. Life mastery is learning to listen to your heart and treating fear voices as considerations rather than fortune tellers.

I wish I could tell you that I bravely sprang into action, but the truth is much different. I hesitated. I slept on it. I attempted to talk myself out of it. I reached out to friends and tried to get them to talk me out of it.

It's important to note here:

This is why it is so crucial to have a 'why' behind anything you do. A 'why' that is much greater than yourself.

If I did not have a 'why' or if my 'why' was nothing more than something self-centered like: "it'll give me something to do," I would not have taken the actions I did. Instead, I would have allowed fear to decide for me and retreated to the safety of what's familiar.

But because my 'why' was less about me and more about you, I decided to ask.

I published a Facebook post that essentially asked for help. I asked if experts in fields such as healing, mindset, accounting, legal, finance, faith, mental health, business, digital marketing, etc. would be willing to be interviewed by me and share some of their expertise (which I call magic) with you.

The experts would not be allowed to pitch or sell. There wouldn't even be an email list built for which they could market to later. This was purely about heartfelt giving.

The best-case scenario I imagined was finding 10 people who were willing to do this. The reality was far different. Nearly 30 people responded within the first 24 hours, either offering their own magic or recommending someone who might be open to offering theirs.

The first interviews were scheduled to begin two days later.

The name of the series 'A Handful of Hope' was decided by myself and the first guest, Alisha Joy, a few minutes before we began recording her interview.

There were dozens of things I did not know how to do; proper lighting, converting audio files, whether I needed a website, or how to organize this. However, I found that when you have a clear why, who, what and how, you do not need to know all those other details to begin. All you need to do is start the process and trust in what your heart is saying.

With so many incredible people willing to participate, some of whom are fellow authors in this book, the process quickly evolved. From what started as interviews, heart to heart conversations with fellow human beings who wanted to share their magic and support others, began to form.

It quickly took on a life of its own as guests began recommending friends who they believed would be great additions. In the first month I recorded more than 60 interviews. We will surpass 100 by the middle of May.

The videos are being shared Monday to Friday on both my various social media platforms as well as the temporary website I threw together (I turned a "leadpage" into a website as a quick work around).

People have been requesting a podcast version which just became available on Apple/Stitcher/Spotify.

I'm looking into improving the overall production quality of the podcast to make it as helpful and accessible as possible. (If you are interested in investing in the funding of a higher quality 'A Handful of Hope' podcast, please don't hesitate to message me).

Writing to you now, I can honestly say that this period of 'sheltering in place' has been one of the most enriching, joy filled and purpose driven periods of my life. I haven't been obsessing over how to get more clients, how to improve my biz, how to reach more people and wondering what's going to happen to me, (all of which are, when you dig deep, fear-based obsessions). Instead, my single obsession has been focused on how we can put a more generous 'Handful of Hope' into the world today?

I've been blessed to meet some of the most incredible

human beings – many of whom I did not know before March, but now consider lifelong friends.

This period of time, just like any period of life, has not been perfect. It has had its share of challenges. However, despite the challenges it has been pretty damn crazy amazing. Crazy amazing does not mean crazy perfect.

The series is called 'A Handful of Hope'. To me it has honored that name. Every time I have a conversation with one of the magic makers, I find my heart overflowing with hope for the future that we can build together.

It all begins with a decision.

Right now, my dear friend, you too have an opportunity to make a decision. What you decide will determine your destiny. Look into your heart… what is there? Trust in what you see and make your decision based on that. Your heart will lead you to the destiny that you are meant to live.

Carpe Diem & with love,
Jesse

6

Sparkling in The Midst of Insanity

— By Michelle Eades —

"Don't Stop Me Now" by Queen is blasting in my ears as I begin to write. It's my "Sparkle Strategy" today. So. Much. FUN! It's impossible to sit still and I feel inclined to jump out of my seat to dance (like nobody's watching) around the room. *This* is what Sparkling in the Midst of Insanity looks like in my world!

The Insanity

I feel a little sad which is pretty good, actually, because I have felt *very* sad over the weeks of isolation due to the coronavirus. How hard is it to be told you can't leave home except for essential food shopping and exercise? And, how easy is it to get depressed and feel sad (and angry)? I've had days of big emotion followed by days of less emotion, days of being quite okay followed by days of being totally not okay, on repeat. I'm pretty sure that a lot of people have experienced something similar.

I'm now sharing my normally quiet home with my daughter, my husband, and my son who recently moved home for awhile. We do have a big house, but four adults living together is a very different reality from living as a family with three dependent children. There were the mental and emotional challenges of my husband being asked to work from home, but my son was still able to go out to work. There was the 'parental distress' of having two of my kids at home with us while one was not. There was the question of whether my daughter see her boyfriend (who was also still working outside of the home), what were the rules around that and then, the emotional impact of people seeing things differently and interpreting rules in different ways. Yep, insanity.

I learned, pretty quickly, that the only thing I had any control over were *my* feelings and *my* responses. I do feel a little bit badly that it has taken me so long to get all that worked out. I thought about the fact that the pandemic life we've been living is a brand new experience. Nobody knows how to do this life, nor how to do it well. Grace!

The one thing that has really helped me is a strategy from my JOYFUL WARRIORS Card Deck: "Practice your SPARKLE Face!" Little did I know, when I was gathering strategies for managing my anxiety, that this one would become my favorite.

"When you are in Sparkle-mode, you can feel it. It's like you have fairy lights shining from your eyes and you can almost see the JOY Bubbles dancing around you." JOYFUL WARRIORS Guidebook page 90.

Back in the day, when I was navigating a path where I lived with anxiety, I collected tools and strategies that could help me feel safer. I needed practical actions I could take in order to be able to function well in the outside world. I am incredibly grateful for that journey because those strategies and tools are at my fingertips, right in the front of my mind, ready to go when I am in need. Fortunately, that need has lessened over the years. Even more fortunately, those strategies are still there during this time of isolation and I am using them every day.

I don't suffer from anxiety much anymore. But that anxiety has reached out to me throughout isolation. It usually turns up in the form of acute distress about the state of the world or when I have simply been doing too much and feel overwhelmed. My need to help and be of service has increased dramatically, especially in my virtual communities. I have been doing virtual gatherings of varying sorts up to three times a week, interspersed with one-on-one video conversations. I've been living in multiple time zones and unsure of what my 'normal' schedule actually looks like.

The anxiety shows up as lots and lots of tears, seeming to pour out of my eyes even when I don't think I'm that distressed. The more I try and make things easier for others, the harder it gets for me.

"When you are Starting Out you might be a little perplexed about this concept. If you haven't had someone show you a Sparkle Face or comment when you are wearing one, you might not know exactly what it is. So, you'll need to think about what ingredients go into forming the Sparkle image." JOYFUL WARRIORS Guidebook page 91.

Finding My Sparkle

I have a collection of 'sparkly' lipsticks and lip glosses, and I have a drawer full of bubble blowing paraphernalia. At the time I was creating my card deck, sparkly lipstick as a fashion statement was trending. Unicorns had become the 'big thing' and, as a result, you could purchase "Unicorn Lipstick". This tickled my fancy in a big way. As I remember discovering that first sparkly lipstick, I find myself grinning. The next time I was out shopping I found sparkly lip gloss. As one who'd not worn lip gloss in about thirty years, this was a very exciting experience for me. I bought two colours, Pink Slip and Blue Sky, playing with them after getting home, taking selfies on my phone so I could see what they looked like, and commenting on how scrumptious they tasted. I was in Sparkle Heaven! I now have five different Sparkle Lip Indulgences and they sit on my desk ready for when I need a Sparkle Boost.

The other thing which brings me Great JOY is blowing bubbles. Another strategy from the JOYFUL WARRIORS Card Deck that came in the form of "JOY Bubbles". This is that feeling you get when the JOY literally bubbles up from the depths of your being. It feels like soda bubbles.

I remembered having a lot of fun as a kid, blowing bubbles. When I was struggling to find ways to live better with anxiety, I remembered the fun of bubbles. I remembered the ways that different wand shapes blew different sized bubbles. I remembered bubble baths filled to overflowing with white fluffy bubbles, and gathering a handful of them and clapping my hands together. Bubbles sprayed everywhere!

"That feeling when you have to laugh and you try not to, you push it down, kind of holding your breath, but it keeps fizzing until it explodes in a loud outburst … just like when you shake up a soda bottle.

JOY Bubbles!

An Eruption of JOY Bubbles!"

JOYFUL WARRIORS Guidebook page 73.

Sparkly lipstick and blowing bubbles are my 'go to' actions when I am feeling in need of a boost in energy or a refresh in attitude. They have been essential tools in my Isolation period.

Seeking Sparkle and JOY Bubbles

The gift of being in isolation and having to navigate a new normal is finding new ways to connect with my Sparkle Self.

The first step in the process was to have a sit-down

conversation with my house mates. They needed to understand that my world, working from home, and their worlds, working outside our home, wouldn't both work in our new reality. That was a conversation with a lot of honesty and a lot more awareness around the differences between our work worlds. We talked and shared and explored and compromised. We created a Workday Plan, where my husband still kissed me goodbye as he went to work (fifteen steps away rather than an hour's drive) and kissed me when he 'got home'. We also allowed for the daily movements and interactions which would need 'tweaking' as we went along.

Phew! First challenge addressed. First sense of security and structure achieved. Goodbye Anxiety.

Next, I worked out how to have structure in my world, now that there were many more 'outside' distractions. My daughter and I had started this process a few weeks before while she, too, was working from home. We decided to have "Work Coffees". Once a week, we would go to our favourite café and buy our favourite drinks then sit and work while we drank them. It was a lot of fun because it was unusual for me in my regular work world. We went on a bit of an adventure seeking out all the options of iced coffees until we discovered 'the one' that was exactly right.

Then the pandemic arrived, and we were asked to stay home, only going out to buy essentials. One of our early shopping trips involved popping into the store to buy fancy glasses (inspired by the ones our favourite café used) and metal straws.

I also indulged in some pretty serviettes and paper doilies. That was a Fun Shopping Trip and filled with lots of Sparkle!

Our first Isolation Work Coffee was in my workspace, at my table. We replicated, as best we could, our favourite iced drinks, served them on little plates with a doily, and placed a table number on the side. So. Much. Fun!

We had worked out how to replicate the outside world in our isolation world. Sparkle energy and JOY bubbles abounded!

Now that we had addressed the new dynamic isolating at home and created some structure, bringing in some of the magic from our non-isolation life, it was much easier to find other little things that brought in Sparkly Feelings and fed my JOY.

Moments which have brought me JOY and lifted the insanity of the pandemic world have included walking around my garden, pulling weeds, watching flowers bloom, and running my hand over aromatic leaves then deeply inhaling the scent. Bringing in bunches of greenery, herbs and pretty branches to put in a vase in my workspace has been a complete JOY.

We have planned our meals in much greater detail than ever before. There has been time and space to think about what we'd really love to eat, and the opportunity to create different meals. We visited the Asian Supermarket and bought a variety of foods that we'd always wanted to try or looked interesting. We cooked together, and we ate dinner together. There have been some fabulous conversations about what foods or recipes we want to try next. Variety of foods, random mealtimes, sitting at different places around the table, and homemade snacks have brought a lot of fun and 'sparkle' into my day.

Life is not always easy. Pandemic life seems rarely be easy. It's not always straightforward to bring Sparkle into the day. Those moments when it all seems too hard and you have no energy left—when your ability to roll with the punches and 'turn the other cheek' is non-existent, they're the hardest of all. It seems like nothing will ever change and you might never leave your house again. Those are the days when I simply go back to bed.

Going back to bed because the world is too hard usually involves putting on my favorite, comfortable pajamas. I grab bed socks and my husband's cuddliest sweater. I throw my favorite blanket on top of the bedclothes and get the extra cushions ready. Finally, I gather up my stuffed animal toy, a plush Winnie-the-Pooh gifted to me by my gorgeous husband at the birth of our first child, and push him under the covers. I climb into bed and create a nest. The covers are pulled up over my ears, Winnie-the-Pooh is placed so his head aligns with my heart, and the cushions are piled so high around me they make a little cave.

No matter what the weather is like outside, this is my 'pull the covers over my head' ritual. If it's hot, I turn on the air conditioning. I close all the blinds and the doors, and I huddle with my dearest comfort companion and go to sleep. The world seems just a little bit easier after I have slept.

Oh! Did you notice? Did you see what I did?

I created SPARKLE even in a time of craziness.

- Favorite pyjamas.
- Cuddly blanket and cushions.

- Husband's sweater.
- Stuffed Toy.
- Created a cave in which to hibernate.

Even when it seems like the insanity is overtaking my life I can create a little bit of Sparkle in the most unlikely of places.

7

Finding a New Normal

— By Dr. Brittany Fernandez —

"Oh, it's so refreshing to sleep in on a clinic day", I thought to myself as I poured a cup of coffee into my 'Bee Happy' mug instead of my usual to-go cup that I forget to securely seal a quarter of the time. During the first few days of quarantine I was relieved to enjoy a workday that didn't start at 5am. It was nice to make breakfast and eat at the kitchen table, rather than take a quick bite for the road. Initially, I immersed myself in home life. Disappointingly, my freshly washed pajama bottoms and a t-shirt became my new attire and days quickly became sedentary. Not to mention, the cold, dark, rainy weather that catered to the idea of staying in bed. This less than productive lifestyle became the new normal, and I found myself feeling unmotivated and blue. I needed to more intentionally put my talents to use. Like most, I was primarily in disbelief that in the 21st century we were suffering from a global pandemic. The solitude that resulted, attempted to manipulate my psyche, and I didn't want my patients, especially those who had been more significantly affected, to let it get the best of them.

I became angry that the pandemic restricted my face-to-face visits with patients. I felt that our patients deserved more from their physicians. I experienced a sense of guilt, then acceptance and motivation to make a difference in my patients' lives and focus on improving patient care. Looking back, I found myself going through something similar to the stages of grief. I imagined that my patients were likely experiencing paralleled emotions, perhaps worse. Like many, some patients have been furloughed from work, some have gained the responsibility of caring for loved ones who were financially or physically affected and some are trying to juggle working from home while raising children, all while making sure their schoolwork is completed. My job as a physician includes focusing on the mental and physical wellbeing of every patient that walks through the door. I have been referring to the last few 'shelter in place' months as a *season*, and this is a scary one. I find myself telling my patients that this is just a moment in time, which just like any season, won't last forever. My encounters are prepped by changing my mask and gloves before the start of our visit, cleaning my stethoscope, interviewing and examining each patient as quickly and as effectively as possible, and asking about their wellbeing. How have they been affected? How are they coping? Are they feeling sad or discouraged? Our visits are quick and concise, but by the end, I have a sense of how unnerving this experience has been, if at all. I share that my daily mantra includes, "today I am grateful." It may seem simple, but on the days that are long and taxing, it may not be as easy as you think. Reflecting on the joy and gratitude of my day translates to a happier, more productive, more encouraging and optimistic version of myself. Practicing gratitude has made it increasingly possible to reveal the positivity that surrounds me. I challenge my patients to find one thing they are grateful for each day. I started doing this after it was recommended by my Aunt Ann Marie. It has since enriched my life. If it helps one person, then I have succeeded.

As a physician, this time has brought on lots of uncertainty, fear and intimidation, both professionally and personally. I am currently the Chief Resident of a residency program in Southern California. I am not only concerned for my patients and their families, but for my fellow residents as well. I take my family into consideration, as I do theirs. We have residents who have children, some who live with their parents, some with comorbid conditions, some caring for immunosuppressed family members and some with pregnant siblings or spouses. I have made it my responsibility to check in with everyone…what are they doing for fun? To stay safe? It is easy to let friendships fall between the cracks, especially when we are all fighting against this beast of a virus and may be mentally and/or physically exhausted. The dismal idea of social distancing alone can make the days seem longer and more desolate for anyone. One thing I've taken away from this experience is, if you can, make it a point to check in with those around you. I have made it part of my daily routine to connect with a colleague, a relative or a distant friend. Although social media is often an easy outlet and approach to unite one another, I challenge you to think about grandma who may not have a smart phone, much less know how to use one. Wave at a stranger walking their dog (I hope they are walking 6 feet from you). Leave a bottle of water for your mail carrier with a simple note that says, "Thanks for all you do! Stay safe!" Whether it's sending a simple text to say hello, messaging someone on social media, writing a "just thinking of you" card or calling in a greeting to someone who lives alone, let that person know that you appreciate them and care about how they are doing during this season. It's free, and I guarantee it will brighten their day.

I was certain 2020 would be a memorable year for me, and this experience has only made it a more remarkable one. My husband and I purchased our first home, I am on track to finishing up my residency program in June and we are looking forward to traveling and exploring more of the world together. We have definitely made memories during the last couple of months and have laughed along the way. By quarantine day 12 I was starting to feel antsy. Now what?! Initially it was comforting to spend the day in pajamas, but I reached a point where I questioned, "Who does this really benefit?" Although I am fortunate enough to have an essential job, my daily routine had been thrown off, and I was starting to feel it. Since my husband has been working from home since mid-March, I think he was starting to feel it too. They say it takes 2 weeks to form a habit, and I didn't want sleeping in, followed by catching up on a Netflix series to be my new one. I could not be more thankful that our new little casita is a 'fixer upper'. Not to mention, we needed new furnishings to fill it with. I always love a good bargain, so I was eager to start my hunt for dining chairs to go with our new mid-century dining table. Luckily, I found a good deal from a local shop's online sale section and placed my order. I will be honest, I was rather overwhelmed with the three giant rectangular boxes that arrived. I am not normally the hands-on-construction-loving-volunteer-to-put-something-together type of person. However, this time was different. With the extra time I had, I willingly began to assemble the six new chairs I had found. Although it took me a couple of days, or four or five, I was quite proud of myself once they were successfully built. If you have been contemplating a purchase, my suggestion is to try and shop at local, small businesses. I know there are a lot of small business owners struggling during this time, so if it's a coffee from a local café, an item of clothing from your local clothing store or a burger from your favorite restaurant, remember to support small business owners and their staff. I have taken this time to direct my focus on how to improve myself and support my community. Not only did I put the chairs together, but I sprayed them with scotch guard to protect the fabric. After that, I walked through our home and painted over ever small chip in paint, fastened every outlet, arranged closets, and am currently working on organizing the garage. We have tangerine and lemon trees that are flourishing with fruit in our backyard, so I made goodie bags for family members with the hope of putting a smile on their face. Need something to keep you busy during this time? Find something at home that needs organization, assembly, or fixing! I promise you will feel a sense of accomplishment once your task is complete!

Do something out of the ordinary. Like I said, I am not normally the type of person to want to build something, but I was recently contemplating a Pinterest-inspired project and decided a planter box was just the thing we needed for our new front lawn! Although we are working from home, we are doing just that, working. Jayson, my husband, has created his office in the kitchen and I am both working and studying in the spare bedroom. Constructing a planter box helped break the monotony of daily life in our new office spaces. It was a hands-on project for my husband and I, and we would be able to fill it with lovely flowers that would bring color and happiness to our new 'shelter in place' lifestyle. We took charge of different parts: I sealed the wood and Jayson fastened all the pieces into place. Together we created something beautiful, something we were proud of. I am one of four children, and when I was a little girl, the six of us would sit around the dinner table and my dad would ask, "How was your day?" or "What did you learn today?" No kid likes answering those questions! That was when we started our own tradition, asking each other, "What was the funniest part of your day?" By the time the six of us shared what that was, you would find us laughing so hard we were crying! I am happy that my husband and I continue to practice sharing the funniest part of our day while enjoying the evenings in our yard. We often have dinner on a bistro set we've set out by our planter box covered in blooms. It is important for us to take a moment to join in laughter, sentiment and tradition with those you love. Maybe it's not a planter box that you're into, but rather beautifying your garden, practicing your own traditions, painting, cleaning up the yard, or creating a space to meditate or reflect on what you're grateful for and what puts a smile on your face.

If you know me, you know how important family is to me, it's everything! I talk to my mom every day on the way into work. She is a teacher for LAUSD and likes to leave extra early to beat the L.A. traffic and accomplish a few tasks before her students arrive. Since our work schedules have been shifted a bit, we still make sure to talk daily, just at different times. Like I mentioned, I come from a big family, but I married into an even bigger one. After a while, not seeing everyone was beginning to have an effect on my own wellness. By quarantine day 14 we were well versed in FaceTime family sessions to say hello, celebrate a birthday or enjoy a family meal together. We are still connecting, just in a different way. I am still able to chat it up with my sisters, joke with my brother, watch my nephews grow and reach their age appropriate milestones, enjoy a happy hour with my close girlfriends and even give tours of our new home to cousins, aunts and uncles. My point is, do not let social distancing keep you from those you love. If talking on the phone is not enough, find a way to visit one another.

The possibilities are endless! As a family, we have learned to be creative, have fun and make the best of the situation. We have decided to be stronger than the influences that surround us, and we are much happier for it.

Set a goal. In February, I was *lucky* enough to be randomly selected for the USA Women's Half Marathon in Palm Desert, CA. Lucky as in NOW is my time to train! I don't think I've mentioned it yet, but I have two handsome four-legged boys: Jack (a very distinguished 7 year old maltipoo) and Hudson (a 2 year old silly labradoodle). Jack was made for quarantine life. He takes pride in napping, only stretching his legs for the sound of anything plastic wrapped, thinking it's a treat. Hudson on the other hand enjoys protecting his yard, chasing birds, annoying the squirrels and often gets restless if he has not been on a long hike in a few days. So, Hudson has become my running buddy. By the beginning of mile 3 he starts to slow down, but we enjoy expending our energy together! When I'm not working, studying, finding something to do around the house or running, I've been working on a book about my boys. 'The Adventures of Jack and Hudson' is a book series targeted toward young children. It is meant to be relatable and help them adapt to some of life's challenges. It is my dream for 'The Adventures of Jack and Hudson' to be relevant to today's youth and help aid in the process of adjusting to various situations young children encounter. I know that some of you are probably thinking a children's book series is the complete opposite of medicine, what is she doing? But the creativity behind it has allowed these books to be my escape and has made this season that much more tolerable. Set a goal, no one says you must achieve it tomorrow, in a month or even by this year. If it brings you joy and you are passionate about something you love, do not be afraid to do it. You will get to the finish line.

Like I said, we bought a fixer upper and are currently in the middle of a mainline plumbing emergency. Needless to say, we are thankful to be home. I hope this season has brought you peace, laughter and hope. Although this journey can been difficult at times, I have learned a lot about myself and the things I am grateful for; a supportive family, a loving husband, a home with lots of old charm, our fun puppies, time to study, time to set a goal, to creatively connect with someone and to be present. I have recently been comforted by finding value in the time spent at home, working on a project I would have postponed to a later time, and both defining and fine tuning my self-worth and purpose. For that, I am grateful.

What are you grateful for?

8

A Thousand Reasons to Smile

— By Monica Gonzales —

2020 started off pretty AMAZING. On January 4th 2020 I passed my California Real Estate exam and I was ready to jump in with both feet on this exciting new chapter in my life. By March 1st I had listings valued at over 2.5 million dollars. Just as we were ready to sign the listing agreement and make the listings go live, we were advised by the Governor of California that we were in a pandemic and facing 'stay at home' orders. Hmmm, what did that mean? Businesses were forced to close. People were hoarding toilet paper. With not many details on what lay ahead in the coming weeks, the feeling of uncertainty was great. My home was now my new office, on-line homeschool for my daughter and the word *coronavirus* was something new we were all talking about. There was no time to object to any of the new norms. I quickly had to decide that I would look for the good in all this. How I embrace uncertainty in my life is what leads to great transformations within us, I pondered that thought. I decided at that very moment I was going to use this time in quarantine to the fullest, no matter what. There is no better way to do so than to be of service to others.

I received a call from my sister that she had a very good friend that had just recovered from cancer and was in great need of a face mask due to this COVID-19 outbreak. I had never worn a face mask let alone sewn one. I hung up the phone with my sister and immediately called our mom and said, "Mom, we need to make face masks and we need to make a lot of them." Without any hesitation she said, "YES … YES, count me in". I owned a sewing machine so that was good for starters, but I didn't really know a lot. I researched on the internet what others were doing. I downloaded patterns, watched YouTube tutorials and figured it out. My mom and I were now face mask making machines. I would FaceTime my mom asking for help as I sewed up my first few. Each mask we created has a bigger meaning than just pretty fabric, it was so much more. These masks for the present moment are satisfying a need; a need to protect yourself, a need to protect others and a sense of security that you may just be able to avoid catching this dreadful virus. Most importantly, it felt so good to create something that was needed in such crucial times.

I reflect on the idea that everyday, each one of us is given the opportunity to perform an act of kindness, all at a moment's notice. We are able to come out of our comfort zones and learn new things. When uncertain events take place, we are given a choice to take advantage of the opportunities presented to us, or bury our heads in the sand. Being raised with two of the most generous of parents that lead by example, I was always taught to step up, be the first to volunteer or deliver food to someone in need. This made it inherently easy to say yes to making a face masks. As a mom to a beautiful teenage daughter who is always watching and observing my actions, it was important for me to also lead by example, as my parents did, and show her how we as a family were going to navigate through this pandemic. We can look back and be proud of how we spent this time together or regret we didn't do more. Today's pandemic will pass, life will pick up once again, businesses will reopen and shelves will be stocked high with toilet paper. But what changes did I make? What opportunities did I seize? How did I use my time? Here's my 6-step daily routine on how I've been living a happy quarantined life:

1. **Pray**… Pray often

2. **Be Grateful**… Start your day being very grateful. Feeling this gratitude in my heart that the sun is shining, my heart is beating, I'm safe, I'm healthy, I have a refrigerator filled with food, I have a home, I have a job I love and I have the best family in the world.

3. **Stay Positive**… Change your mindset from 'I'm stuck at home' to 'I am safe at home'. When you practice this, you put yourself in the best position possible to

succeed in tough times, you become a better person in the process. Choose your conversations wisely.

4. **Take up a Hobby**… Dive into something you love. Learn everything about it and share this passion with the world. A wise woman once told me that she has never met anyone suffering from boredom or depression when they occupy their time doing something they absolutely love.

5. **Acts of Kindness**… This is my favorite. Size doesn't matter with this one. Whether it be the smallest or biggest acts of kindness, it is the best gift you can give yourself. Pay for the drink of the person in the car behind you at Starbucks. Give a handwritten card to a friend. Bring in the trash can for an elderly neighbor. The sky's the limit.

6. **Fall in Love with your home**… Cooking as a family has been a daily highlight of mine. Watching my daughter bake up a new recipe she found on Pinterest. Hosting random family dance parties anytime of the day. Movie nights by the fire with a bowl of popcorn.

None of us could have predicted 2020 was going to start off this way. But all of us can decide how we live through it. The choices we make today, opportunities we take advantage of, the positive attitudes we adopt, the kindness we show and the memories we create will far outlast these difficult times.

When life gives you a hundred reasons to cry, show life that you have a thousand reasons to smile.

9

Thriving Through Turbulent Times: 6 Positive Psychology Strategies

— By Iris Polit —

Positive psychology methodologies can be used to thrive through transitions when you are facing one of life's normal transformations, such as a change in your career, facing a divorce, an unexpected health issue, etc. However, how can we thrive when it seems the whole world has turned upside down and we are struggling to cope with a new 'normal'?

To claim that we are going through turbulent times currently would be trite. It would diminish the actual magnitude of our current existence. This new reality has taken individually stressful situations -- such as sickness, furloughs or lay-offs, working remotely, home schooling, isolation and, in some worst cases, death -- and compounded them into one seemingly insurmountable mountain of complex challenges.

When I am confronted with both uncertainly and fear, I rely on knowledge and facts to help me overcome them. Admittedly, for me that means digging into the positive psychology* toolbox, whether it be one specific situation or a multitude of adverse circumstances. I have found that applying various methodologies (based on research and neuroscience) has been very valuable and beneficial.

For those of you not familiar with positive psychology:

"Positive psychology is the scientific study of optimal human functioning. It aims to discover and promote the factors that allow individuals and communities to thrive."

(Seligman, 2002).

Since traditional psychology was based on a disease model – fixing what is wrong with people – the optimal outcome when using this approach would be to reach 'neutral' or not be considered 'sick'. Positive psychology, on the other hand, focuses on getting to the 'north of neutral' and enhancing the positive aspects of people's lives. After all, just because someone is not depressed this does not mean that they are necessarily happy or fulfilled within their lives. Therefore, positive psychology focuses on enhancing well-being and flourishing. In doing so, it aims to create a more balanced psychology that encompasses the wholeness of the human experience.

Just as there are many layers to the challenges we are facing, there are also ways in which we can layer several positive psychology methodologies to help us overcome our challenges.

Although positive psychology is a descriptive (rather than a prescriptive) science, I've found that leaning into its foundational elements (the PERMA-V model of wellbeing) has helped me cope and thrive through these tentative times. I hope it can do the same for you.

The PERMA-V model is comprised of:
- Positivity
- Engagement
- Relationships
- Meaning
- Accomplishment
- Vitality

While there are many intentional activities and strategies attached to each element of PERMA-V, I would like to share a few specific ones that I have used and continue to use, that help me stay sane and potentially thrive.

Positivity – Focus on Gratitude

When it comes to positivity, my go-to is always to focus on gratitude. I've written about the benefits of gratitude previously and it is certainly my top signature strength…one I lean on regularly. However, it is understandable that now, more than ever, it may be a bit difficult to feel as though you have a lot that you 'should' be grateful for, and truly feel authentic gratitude.

Research indicates that "grateful people are more likely to attribute the positive things in their lives to external sources" (McCullough, Emmons & Tsang, 2002). So, when our external world has turned upside down, how can we be grateful? The key is to start small. What are the little things that warm your heart? Is there anyone you may have been taking for granted? Is there anything that may have simply disappeared into your noisy world? Begin by tapping into all your primary senses:

- Sound - Birds chirping outside your window
- Sight - Your child's warm smile
- Smell - Sweet scent of spring blossoms
- Taste - Delicious (or creatively pulled together) home cooked meal
- Touch - Soft feel of a fresh role of toilet paper

How to practice this strategy:

On a daily basis, stop to consider what you are grateful for. This can be done when you first wake up and/or when you are going to sleep (or at any point during your day). Take a few minutes to focus on gratitude and recall a few things or people you are thankful for. Focus on the feelings that these things and people bring. Doing so will help you tap into authentic gratitude. Remember, appreciation intervention significantly boosts your immune system!

Engagement - Meditate

This has been one of the most impactful methodologies for me. As someone who has struggled with establishing a regular meditation practice – barely getting through a 5-minute guided meditation in the past, I can now sit through at least 30 minutes daily (sometimes even 50 minutes on the weekend!) leveraging Vishen Lakhiani's 6 Phase Meditation as a framework (connection, gratitude, forgiveness, visualizing, intention, and blessing).

Along the way, there were many myths about meditation that I had to dispel. The biggest one was that the goal of meditation is to empty your mind of all thoughts and distractions, or to create a state of bliss. Once I dismissed that myth, I was able to embrace meditation as an extremely practical tool.

Scientific studies have found a wide variety of physical and mental health benefits of meditation, including:

- Decreased stress and pain
- Reduced anxiety
- Better immune functions
- More self-awareness and empathy
- Greater alertness, self-esteem and self-regulation
- Increased quality of relationships
- And many more!

How to practice this strategy:

Take a few moments to practice meditation every day. Do not worry if you cannot shut your mind off. Start small with these basic mindfulness practices and applications:

- 5:5:5 Breathing – taking 5 breaths, inhaling for 5 counts and exhaling for 5 counts brings the mind and body into a calmer state
- Progressive Muscle Relaxation (PMR) – go through your body parts (from your toes to your head), alternating between squeezing and relaxing each muscle group
- Loving Kindness Meditation (LKM) – this practice of cultivating compassion and love in the heart calms the

body and boosts your immune system as well as positivity. Learn more and get short scripts <u>here</u>.

Relationships – Do Not Isolate

The topic of responsible social distancing has been at the forefront of discussions recently. I choose to look at it a bit differently. While it is important to practice physical distancing, we can still embrace virtual, social closeness. As someone who has been working remotely for almost a decade, I thought I would be an expert at this. However, I was surprised to discover how much social distancing has impacted me. At the root of it all is isolation and loneliness.

An analysis of 148 studies of social support (Holt-Lunstad, Smith & Layton, 2010) suggests that social isolation increases the risk of death about as much as smoking cigarettes and more so than both physical inactivity or obesity! Other research indicates that when people feel lonely, brain regions that are associated with physical pain are activated. Loneliness prepares the body for some looming threat (Leiberman, et al., 2004; Eisenberg, 2014; Eisenberg, Lieberman & Williams, 2003).

How to practice this strategy:

Find ways to connect. Technological advances have provided us with many ways to practice virtual, social closeness. Here are a few activities that I have found very helpful:
- Virtual coffee breaks with coworkers
- Virtual happy hours and dinners with friends

- Virtual volunteering
- Regularly texting, calling or video chatting with family members
- Sharing funny memes and videos with friends and family

Here are some more activities you can do virtually and a bunch of my favorite ways that others have been practicing closeness across the world:

- Husband sings to wife through nursing home window
- <u>Meeting great grandchild</u> through glass
- Kids play music for elderly neighbor
- Italians making music on balconies
- 9-year old surprised by Hamilton cast
- The magic of Redwood National Park and virtual museum tours and #TogetherAtHome with Chris Martin and One World: Together At Home Broadcast and Andrea Bocelli: Amazing Grace and there are many many more!

Meaning – Volunteer and Donate

You may be thinking, is she crazy? What about social distancing? The great news is that many organizations have worked to create virtual volunteer opportunities. For example, I spent a lovely Sunday afternoon with a group of high school students discussing go-to-market strategies and user personas for a project they were working on via Zoom. It all comes down to engaging with your purpose. Purpose is "stable and generalizable intention to accomplish something that is at once meaning-ful to the self and leads to productive engagement with some aspect of the world beyond the self" (Damon, Menon & Bronk, 2003).

Research indicates that there are many benefits of purpose. Purpose impacts wellbeing by:

- Increasing physical (Parquart, 2002) and mental health (Reker, et al., 1987)
- Enhances resiliency and optimism (Compton, et al., 1996)
- Improves self-esteem (Steger, et al., 2006)

How to practice this strategy:

Stop to reflect on how you can help others during these dif-ficult times...even if it's just <u>sharing a few inspiring messages</u> with girls who aren't able to attend their 'We Are Girls' con-ference. If you cannot identify safe volunteering opportunities, consider donating to worthy causes that are meaningful to you or those that are helping others who are most at risk/in need right now. You'd be amazed at the huge impact even a small donation can make (for example a $25 donation can help feed 2 NYC families for a month through City Harvest or provide 200 meals to neighbors in Austin through Central Texas Food Bank). If you are looking for some ideas, here are a few that I have contributed to recently:

- City Harvest and Central Texas Food Bank
- K9s For Warriors
- Girls Empowerment Network

- Westcave Outdoor Discovery Center
- Art from the Streets
- Blue Note New York Employee Support Fund and Health Alliance for Austin Musicians
- Coronavirus Relief Fund and Project C.U.R.E.

Accomplishment – Incorporate Hope

Incorporating hope may sound a bit "woo woo" but it is a methodology that is extremely helpful during times like these. Much like gratitude, I've also previously written about the benefits of <u>hope</u> which I find to be another one of my top signature strengths. When we are faced with situations that seem out of our control, our self-efficacy (having confidence to take on and put in the necessary effort to succeed at challenging tasks) takes a hit. A sense of hopefulness can help bolster it.

According to Peterson and Seligman (2004) hope and optimism predict many desirable outcomes, including:

- Achievement in all sorts of domains (academic, athletic, military, political, and vocational)
- Freedom from anxiety
- Good social relationships and physical well being

How to practice this strategy:

Hope and optimism correlate with being more likely to actively problem solve and put attention on problem-relevant sources of information (Aspinwall & Brunhart, 1996). This is crucial for thriving during times when we feel like everything is out of our control. Take time to regularly revisit past experiences and successes as they are fertile ground for planting and growing seeds of hope (Lopez, et al., 2004). Ask yourself questions to direct your attention toward hopeful elements of stories and experiences. Here are some questions for accessing more hope:

- What is the best you could hope for in the current situation?
- What excites you about your current opportunities?
- What are your hopes for the future?
- What will motivate you to work towards your future goals?
- What do you hope for your family and friends?

Vitality – Outdoor Time

I feel extremely fortunate that there are many nature trails around Austin that provide opportunities to enjoy outdoor time. I cherish spending time in nature. It has an almost magical impact on my mood and is extremely relaxing. Of course, it's all based on science.

Research indicates that "group walks in nature were associated with significantly lower depression, perceived stress, and negative affect, as well as enhanced positive affect and mental well-being" (Marselle, Irvine & Warber, 2014). So, whenever you have a chance, try to spend a bit of time outside…even if it is just to step out of your front door to look up at the sky.

How to practice this strategy:

Stop to consider what you can do to increase vitality in your life on both a daily and weekly basis. Whether that means going for a walk outdoors, doing a handful of squats while brushing your teeth or eating a healthy meal. Although binging your favorite show might seem less overwhelming right now (I do it too!), taking a moment to engage your vitality will certainly do more to help you thrive in the long run.

As you can see among the strategies above, I heavily rely on human connection, nature and music to thrive through these turbulent times. Those may be interventions that work for you or there may be different ones that would better resonate with and support you. Take some time to consider what helps you thrive and find ways to infuse more of it into your life.

I hope you have found the information in this chapter helpful and that you will utilize these or some of your own ways to thrive through our new 'normal'. Be well and thrive!

*Portions of this chapter have previously appeared in a LinkedIn article, 6 Positive Psychology Strategies for Thriving through COVID-19.

10

Sinking Stillness and Serenity

— By Irene Abbou —

Once in a while, we are given a moment when our hearts soften, and we dare to imagine an even more inspiring existence than we ever have before.

Despite my imagination taking me to dark places during this Covid-19 craziness, this morning was one filled with grace. As I sat weary-eyed warmly wrapped in my pink blanket sipping my coffee, I felt a rush of hope, and dare I say a glimpse of excitement for the near future. It was as if my relentless inner three-year-old who tirelessly pushes me to keep on keeping on, found a moment of the serenity of her own.

The wiser part of me was reminded that with some sinking, stillness, and silence our innate fairy G-D mother has the courage to sit beside us, hold us warmly and show us that life can still be full of magic, even in the midst of uncertainty.

For some, uncertainty looks like the constant chaos of interruptions of stressed out recently unemployed spouses needing a sounding board or kids bouncing off the walls since camp and playdates are a thing of the past. For others, it's the inescapable solitary days on zoom chats and evenings longing for the warmth of a real human body.

I learned an important lesson in the last three months of being confined and not knowing which way was up. I learned I could be creative and resourceful. My new life could still include beautiful moments if I continued focusing first and foremost on the habits that nourished my emotional health. Sure, I'd have to re-arrange my schedule to accommodate my entire family being home 24/7, but I still could practice my self-care rituals, which would give me the energy I needed to feel alive.

When our mind is nourished with daily goodness, we are so much more able to respond with compassion and vitality to all the challenges. Human beings have an incredible superpower we often forget about called hedonic adaptation. This is our capability to return to a stable level of happiness after being served a life-altering over-sized shit sandwich.

Our seemingly secure CEO control over our pre-COVID lives has always been just that…seemingly. If you've ever sat in meditation trying to discipline your thoughts, you'll understand first hand that we are definitely not the CEO of our lives. We're barely the awkward summer intern who keeps getting lost on her way to the bathroom. It is ok to stop frantically rising to try to accomplish as you have before.

I challenge you to try the exact opposite.

Sink.

Twice a day (even once will make a difference) make yourself into a real person again. Find a quiet place to restore your faith. In Nature under a cheerful tree or even securely snuggled in the nook of your bedroom closet. Sink in silence and connect to your body. Listen to the part of you that already knows what is true. You are loved, and we will be ok.

I know we collectively fear the ground beneath us is crumbling. What is really happening in the soil of our overworked earth is resourcing. In this time of rest, she is slowly reclaiming her power to create more fertile earth, fruitful trees, and an even more solid ground for us to feel stable on.

If right now, your logical brain took a trip to Burning Man, leaving you in a mush-brain cabin fever funk, be compassionate with yourself.

If you're feeling scared, angry, or confused.... sink.
If your work-outs have gone to shit ......sink.
If your evening glass of wine has turned into two ..... sink.
If you haven't washed your hair in three days..... sink.

If you have a little more energy in a few days or a couple of hours, it's also ok to take a ten min yoga class on YouTube, start the first page of your book, brainstorm a more exciting career path, or simply take a soothing shower. Warm showers always make such a difference for me when my mind needs a friendly reminder that it's not the boss of me. Do whatever feels right for you at this moment, with an open heart and zero judgment.

When the talking is talked, and the doing is done, everything depends on reconnecting to our true self, and that begins with sinking into stillness to recharge our batteries.

Old unhealthy energy is clearing, new inspiring energy is entering, and beautiful things are on their way to you.

We really are all in this together.

You are not alone!

If you know someone that may feel alone, please reach out and remind them that they are not alone. Let's be there for one another and remember that there is no greater healer than the power of human connection.

Sending Love & Light,
Irene

11

5 Steps to Be Crazy Amazing When Going Through a Difficult Time

— By Whitnie Wiley —

I know difficult times. It's not that I don't think living through a pandemic and economic downturn is not difficult, but as are most things in life, it's all about perspective.

This year—2020—is turning out to be a bear. At the end of 2019, social media memes had us waltzing into to this year with 2020 visions of grandeur dancing in our heads. It was going to be the year of awakening, enlightenment and seeing clearly with our 2020 vision glasses and in a lot of respects it has been exactly that. In others, it's been anything but.

When the National Basketball Association (NBA) made the decision on March 11, to abruptly suspend its season, it set the precedent for all the other sports leagues to do the same as a way of helping to flatten the curve of what was turning out to be a growing global pandemic. In the days that followed, many state and local governments started shutting businesses down as well. Businesses of all kinds, large and small, family owned and conglomerates either volunteered to do their part or were voluntold that they were making the sacrifice for the greater good.

I have to admit, in the beginning, I thought the shutdowns were a gift. We were given the rarely used gift of time and space. Our society, American society that is, and probably much of the developed Western world, is on a constant roller coaster ride, in a never-ending cycle of trying to get to the next big thing. We are enamored with bigger, better, faster.

I admit it, there are times when I fit into that mode as well. But 15 years ago, when my world came to a crashing halt with the sudden and tragic death of my son and a friend of his in a car accident, I was left wondering, what is all the hustle and bustle about in the first place.

At the time of his death, if I had not just had the experiences of the preceding two years, I likely would have drowned my sorrows in a bottle. But in 2003, after a long period of singlehood that I was not enjoying, I found myself on the side of the road in the wee hours of the morning bemoaning my singleness. I wondered what was wrong with me that I couldn't either find a man I liked long enough to get through drinks with or the men I made any headway with were emotionally, if not fully, unavailable.

As I was in the street boohoo crying, I heard a voice I now know to be God say, "Try me. You haven't given me a try. Try me." While I've had many direction altering moments, that encounter resulted in my turning my focus away from my carnal pursuits to instead developing my spiritual side. Because of this encounter and the faith I developed over the subsequent two year, I was able to navigate my son's death in a way I never would have otherwise.

Global Pandemic

Where does our current situation with the global reset or coronavirus rank for you in terms of the worst things that have happened in your life? What perspective have you gained about it? Is it truly tough or is it merely inconvenient? Or somewhere in between?

Whether it is the worst thing ever or not, the good news is that with the right mindset and approach, you can not only survive this, you can thrive through it. Following are five action steps you can take that will help you approach any life challenge with a Crazy Amazing® outcome.

Stabilize Your Situation

When your apple cart has been upset and then your pie burns, it's easy to see those events as indications that your whole world is falling apart. Or at least the meal you are preparing. But in reality, it's just a cart and a pie. Instead of tumbling out of control, it's best to stop and take a deep breath to get your bearing about you. Once you've done that, you can begin to assess the damage in real terms, not simply from an emotional place.

Start by asking questions. What is the damage? What is the situation? If you can calmly assess, then you can calmly address. This first step of stabilizing the situation goes a long way toward getting the outcome you deserve. Further, ask for help where necessary and be willing to be a help and resource for others in return.

Determine desired outcome

Speaking of desired outcomes, that is your next step—figuring out what you want at the end. Jack Canfield, bestselling author of the "Success Principles," lays out a principle that says the event plus your response to it creates the outcome you seek. The equation is written as E+R=O. In essence this means that things happen in life that you will not be able to control. However, you can always control your response to events that happen and if you'd like a different outcome you have to learn to respond differently.

As it relates to the difficult time we are going through at the moment, you have the ability to choose how you see the situation, as well as, how you are going to respond to it. Focusing on the outcome you want at the end of this time, will in turn dictate how you choose to respond.

Be Grateful

Being thankful, living in a state of gratitude, is one of the best things you can do in times of challenge or crises. Gratitude is an emotion that helps you gain and maintain perspective. While it takes practice, if you determine to do so, you can always find the good in a situation or something for which to be grateful.

At my son's memorial service, I found myself acknowledging the pain I was in, but, simultaneously I was also in a profound state of gratitude for the opportunity to be his mother and all the love and joy he had brought to my life. That feeling overwhelmed me so much that I rose in the middle of the service to address the attendees to tell them what I was feeling.

Since that time, I have accepted if I could find gratitude in my deepest despair, there is little else that would keep me from feeling, expressing and living in a continuously grateful state.

Remove focus off self

One of most challenging aspects of dealing with trials and challenges is to shed the feeling that somehow life is conspiring against you. It has been proven that the more you can focus on serving the needs of other people the more likely you are to not spiral down a rabbit hole of despair.

The manner in which you choose to serve is irrelevant, what is important is that you identify a need and bring your talents, skills and heart to bear.

Take one step after another

After getting your head screwed on right and figuring out what you want at the end of any particular trial, taking one step after another is the best thing you can do. One of the reasons I've been as successful as I've been and gotten through the rough times, is that I am simply not willing to quit.

My path has often been riddled with obstacles, generally of my own making. Along with the obstacles, however, were opportunities for great learning. Knowing that has given me the hope I have needed to keep going. I've learned to zig as well as zag, always with my eyes on the goal, much like a running back heading toward the end zone.

People fail to reach their desired results for two reasons, failure to launch and failure to stay the course. When failure is not an option, you find a way to get started and the reasons to keep going.

It boils down to mindset. The beauty of mindset is that it is available to you when you need it, particularly when the cards are stacked against you. However, it's important to note for your mindset to serve you in your hour of need, you have to have developed the habit or practice of keeping it positive.

A positive mindset is like a muscle that you build through repetition of large and small lifts. To develop a mindset that will serve you, you need to have called on it for big challenges as well as little ones along your journey. It is this accumulation of experiences that you will call on to help you push or pull through.

Let's take the current environment we're in with the closures of businesses and services along with the stay at home orders. At the start of the shelter in place orders, many people who were not deemed essential, were either let go or converted to remote work. Because I'm self-employed, I wasn't at risk of losing my job per se, although opportunities were lost in the early days as we transitioned from in-person, on location events to virtual ones.

Neither was I affected by working from home, because that was my status quo for 18 months. In fact, I'd had opportunity to work from home sporadically throughout my career, so when I originally transitioned to my home office, I knew what to expect and had formulated an attitude and mindset around it. That made it possible for me to be a resource to others as they began working at home for the first time. In reality, obstacles, challenges, trials, tests, whatever you want to call them are simply opportunities if you've set your mind to view them that way.

Conclusion

When something happens and up ends your life as you know it, take the time to assess the situation and see what you are up against, what you are working with. Breathe, figure out what you are feeling, then once you've done that it's time to move into action mode. Make a decision as quickly as possible on the outcome you'd like to see as a result of this new circumstance. Then begin looking for the good in what's happening, the things you can learn lesson from and be grateful for. Approaching your situation with a grateful heart removes the fear and any doubt that may be developing about whether you can handle what's before you.

Another result of being grateful is that you can focus on other people. The benefit of which is that you won't then obsess over what is happening. Serving others is practical and centering, but this is not to be done until you have assessed your situation and stabilized it. Remember the admonition to put your own oxygen mask on first, then help others.

And then finally after setting up to move on, it's time to take your first step forward following up each step with just one more step. It is this one step after another approach that will ultimately have you looking backward and seeing how far you've traveled and knowing you were crazy amazing through a difficult time.

12

Enjoy the journey

— By Jocelyn Kuhn —

I f there is one thing I know for sure, it's that none of us escape this life without experiencing difficult days. As a child, my mom would often say to us kids, "If all the world's problems were thrown into a hat, you'd gladly take yours back very quickly." While my cynical teenage self used to question whether or not that sentiment was actually true, I saw enough pain and suffering in the world to surmise that she was probably right. I had no idea the pain that was to come in my life, or that looking back to my teenage years now, they'd seem like icing on a really beautiful, delicious cake. How was I to know then that everything that I thought was my life would be completely destroyed in the blink of an eye?

In the course of a five year period; I found out my dad was living a double life, I became unexpectedly pregnant at 19, gave birth to two boys before my 21st birthday, sat in a court-room watching my dad get sentenced to five years in Federal Prison, saw my little brother lay in a bed in the ICU after at-tempting to take his own life, got divorced from my babies' father and finally, as if that weren't already enough, found my dad dead on my couch the weekend before he was supposed to turn himself in to serve his sentence. It's a long story for anoth-er day, but over the course of those five years, I realized exactly what my mom was talking about. I wished so badly to go back to the naivety of my younger self, but even still, I knew she was right—if the world's problems were thrown into a hat, despite all I had been through, I'd gladly take mine back.

Fast forward to 2010. There was this incredible movie that hit the big screen. You may know it. It was based on Elizabeth Gilbert's book, *Eat, Pray, Love*. It was kind of a big deal. In the book there is a beautiful quote by Elizabeth Gilbert that I have clung to tightly during my darkest days, "Ruin is a gift. Ruin is the road to transformation."

I had never thought about it like that. I was broken, but being broken, it turned out, was *the gift*. There have been many moments over the past twelve years that have allowed me to see this gift in action.

One day, upon returning to work after my dad's funeral, I was having a really difficult moment. I had one of my favorite clients in my chair and I was leaning her back to wash her hair when I completely lost it. I was shocked as she shared with me for the first time in the almost two years I'd known her, that she had lost her son when he was three years old.

PERSPECTIVE. "Yep… I'd definitely take my problems back," I thought. I had two beautiful, healthy boys at home, and as much as I'd experienced pain in losing my dad, I also felt so blessed to get to be a mom to these two precious souls. As our conversation progressed, she shared with me one of the best pieces of advice I've ever received—not a day had gone by in the 40 years since she lost her son that she didn't think about him, but on her worst, most painful days, the thing that got her through it was doing something kind for someone in his honor.

KINDNESS. I immediately put her advice into action. I had heard about a young girl in our community who had cancer, so I asked the salon owner if we could hold a benefit night for her. From there we raised money and formed a non-profit so that we could remodel their family's house. My life was completely changed. Now, even after the pain has subsided, every year my siblings and I meet on the day our dad died at one of his favorite restaurants and write letters to other families in the community who've lost their dad. I know he'd be proud, and it feels good to honor him in this way.

When my dad was going to be going to prison, we decided it would be cool to write a book together about our healing journey. It was going to be called *Letters to the Inside*, both because I was going to be writing to him while he was in prison, and to represent the internal journey of healing and forgiveness. Unfortunately, that book was never written. For a long time I wondered what it could've been and I even thought about writing the book on my own about my healing journey, but the further away from the pain I got, the more it became clear—that book wasn't mine to write.

Nevertheless, I still had a burning desire to become a writer, even if only for myself. I wanted to prove to myself I could do it. I'd sit down to write, but the words just wouldn't come. A few times I got several pages in, but would lose interest. It just didn't feel right. For a while I stopped trying all together. It was during this time that I really dove into my own self-discovery. I read books by people like Tony Robbins, Jack Canfield and Danielle LaPorte. By changing my mindset and my habits, my life completely changed. Over the course of 10 years I've probably read close to 1000 books, but there was one that changed my life more than all the rest: *The Magic* by Rhonda Byrne. It provided an easy to follow, step by step path to a magical life through the power of gratitude.

GRATITUDE. If there was only one piece of advice I could give to someone who wanted to be Crazy Amazing during difficult times, it would be this: Get grateful! More than anything else I've focused on in my life, in both the good times and the more challenging ones, gratitude has had the most profound impact of all. You could say it's had a magical impact. The more you can actively feel grateful for everything, the more you open yourself up to all the blessings that life has to offer.

While this can be challenging during the difficult times, if you look hard enough, there is ALWAYS something to be grateful for. Find it. Feel it. It will change your life. I know this is a bold claim, but I believe with every fiber of my being that gratitude changes everything.

I digress. Back to wanting to write a book… I had this burning desire to write a book, but for years I just couldn't make it happen, until one day, it was as if my soul suddenly said, "It is time." In what felt like an instant, the theme and all the content became clear as day, and the words just flowed out onto the page. I was in a mastermind at the time, and my coach challenged me to have the book finished and published in 90 days. Now that was a new challenge. But everything about it just felt right. 91 days later I had finished my first book, *Thriving Through Transitions*.

TIMING. This leads me to the last piece of wisdom I'd like to leave you with. It's so important to remember that life is a journey, and sometimes there are things we need to work through, heal, and learn from before we move onto the next step. I truly believe that my book was written at exactly the time it was meant to be. I needed to go through all the lessons. I needed to heal. I needed to be the student before I could become a teacher. And now, as I continue to grow, should I decide to write another book, it will be when the timing is right—when I have something of value to say that someone needs to hear. Until then, the timing is always right to keep growing, giving and loving.

As a human race, we are in the midst of a difficult situation, and some of us are going through it on a very personal level, but one thing I know for sure is that we always have a choice in how we respond. None of us escape this life without difficulty or hardship, but we can face it head on and be CRAZY AMAZING!

13

Building a Resilient Mindset

— By Jake Sperley —

I f you'd have asked me in December 2019 whether I was good at handling adversity, I would have pointed you to the eight businesses that I created by the age of 22. I would have told you that despite having moved 19 times I continued hustling, learning, and developing. I may have shared that my parents have eight divorces between them, and that my mother has struggled with alcoholism. I would have assured you I was resilient, maybe not as a conscious choice but as a matter of survival. Then 2020 arrived and knocked me on my ass. At times I've been reduced to tears, yet the year has also revealed itself to be the greatest teacher.

Early Trial And (lots of) Error

My early childhood felt blissful. We lived in a beautiful suburban house, my mom drove a fancy SUV and my dad was a respected critical care physician at the top of his game. We had a pool, and more importantly I had my own candy drawer. One day when I was six I was stunned to learn it was all going away. I understood divorce only as a six year old can - I was upset, remember feeling lost, and at times hopeless. As much as I loved all of those things as a child, as an adult I now recognize that this distress has served me far better than the extravagance of my early childhood. While I still feel for the kid whose world was shattered, I wish that I could go back to my early self to suggest that life was going to be fine and that it was actually working for him.

After my parents divorce, it became apparent that if I needed something, I was going to have to find it, earn it, or win it. Having businesses fed my need to gain my parents praise and attention, while gaining some much desired extra money. My first idea was to create duct tape wallets. The raw material was cheap, and I had nothing but time. This passion moved onto paracord accessories and selling candy bars out of my backpack. Meanwhile, I was raising pigs and chickens for 4H. When a high school art class uncovered a knack for pottery, I started a business making mugs for a local brewery. I then took notice of classmates buying pricey red bull drinks at a drive thru coffee stand each morning before school. That was a simple winner - I undercut the market and made them more convenient by mixing my own supply on campus. Along the way these experiments in retail gave me useful lessons about profit margins, labor costs, and effective advertising. They also helped me earn the badge of being an entrepreneur. Most importantly, they gave me confidence and helped me earn others' respect.

Wanting to find more profitable businesses often fueled my early transitions between ventures. Occasionally businesses being an outright failure forced change. A flop of a drop shipping business taught me a lesson about quick fixes and easy money. I was assured of a six figure income and naively went ahead with an investment in a shopify site with apparel designs. When the customers didn't arrive in waves I had to reconcile with the fact that I had been deceived.

These early business experiments kindled by optimism for a future winner - I could taste long term success. Capitalizing on the exploding food cart scene, I jumped in with both feet. One food truck led to two which then led to a full blown catering company. Perhaps tainted by high school humor I chose to name the business *Sausage King*. Ultimately I should have chosen a name with better lasting power. Here came another very important lesson - hiring friends is often a poor business decision. After growing the business to be a moderate success with multiple food trucks and a brick and mortar presence I sold it. Leveraging the experiences and connections made with this business helped me launch the next venture, *Fair and Event - * Marketplace & Software (www.fairandevent.com).

The idea for Fair and Event was born out of the headaches that I experienced as a vendor at various organized events. The registration process was terribly outdated, disorganized, and wholly ineffective - both for vendors and events. While researching solutions I was stunned that there were no comprehensive tools to streamline the registration and record keeping process. This was clearly a need. I leveraged my connections and found a developer and was appointed to our local fair board to better understand the inner workings and constraints of events. Just as the software completed beta trials and was headed for launch Covid-19 arrived!

2020

On January 23rd, after finding my father barely responsive at his home, an ER doctor told me he was in severe renal and liver failure. His potassium was at dangerously high levels and chances of survival were not in his favor. It was quickly determined that his condition exceeded the capabilities of the regional medical center and he was subsequently rushed to a top tier ICU in a major city.

Not knowing what was ahead, I immediately took family leave from a day job and set my businesses aside. Over the next two months I did what little I could to assist in his recovery. From trying to make sense of morning medical rounds, to staying late at night to ensure a smooth transition from any shift changes. Intubated, and heavily medicated, all I wanted was to be able to exchange "I Love You's" one more time. I didn't miss a day, and there were lots!

While the experience was horrific (mostly for him), I

discovered an incredible gift. As a retired physician my father had worked with and trained a number of the doctors that were now caring for him. They told me stories of how he had shaped their careers and changed their lives while sacrificing for the better of his patients. While I have always had a profound respect for the work he contributed to society, I emerged with a deeper appreciation for the man I have the honor of calling my dad.

Ever so gradually he began to recover. However, it became clear that he would need months of rehabilitation to even have the chance of living independently. Just as we began to explore options a Covid-19 cluster was announced at a facility in the Seattle area. After spending several weeks at a rehab facility we made the decision to take a chance and get him home. Simultaneously, other parts of my world began to collapse. I was laid off from my day job due to a dramatic downturn in revenue as the State stay-at-home mandate went into effect. Shortly thereafter my longtime girlfriend and I split and my grandmother passed away. My life felt like it was in shambles and the business that I recently founded was beginning to suffer. The global pandemic had put a halt to events and it felt like cruel irony that I would have chosen the one industry most impacted.

I'd be lying if I said that those weren't the toughest months of my life. I frequently repeated to myself: "you've survived 100% of your worst days." I also consciously chose to reframe my circumstances. This would create opportunity, it was up to me to find it. Freed up from other demands, I was able to spend three months in home quarantine helping my father in his recovery. This free time also allowed me to think a ton about my business. The "progress" I was expecting to make this year has looked very different for both my business and my personal life, but it has taught me the following three invaluable life strategies I want to share with you.

Three Strategies

1. FOCUS ON FINDING THE OPPORTUNITY

How we interpret the events that happen in our lives can leave us feeling either empowered or helpless. If you find yourself in the doldrums about a situation in your life, remember that you have the ability to swap out the lenses that you view your life through. This takes practice, but pausing and recognizing a negative mindset is a great first step.

- Separate the events in your life from your feelings about them. Don't let others label the events in your life as good or bad for you. Listening to the Story of the Chinese Farmer (https://www.youtube.com/watch?v=OX0OARBqBp0&vl=en) will help drive this point home.
- There is opportunity in every situation. Most recently I heard the statement "Don't waste a good pandemic!". Perhaps it's unexpected, or takes you down an unplanned route, but there's opportunity.
- If you see opportunities and find yourself saying no, you're likely limiting your potential. Or, intentionally

killing a good idea because you are fearful of the unknown. I elected to start the *Against All Average* podcast with business teacher Kyle Tolzman. While I didn't have any experience with podcasts, and certainly lacked initial confidence about how much I might be able to bring to the table, I silenced those doubts and took a leap. This was a fabulous decision for me. I've now met so many INCREDIBLE folks who constantly inspire me. It's also why I have the honor of writing this chapter for you! Please, challenge yourself to say yes to something that scares you. I'd love to hear the result.

2. YOU'VE SURVIVED 100% OF YOUR WORST DAYS

Perspective is key. When I am unsure of a particular life challenge I remind myself that if I survived yesterday, and today, why can't I survive tomorrow? The point being, you've survived 100% of the worst days in your life. Have courage knowing that adversity has strengthened you, and prepared you for the hurdle of today.

- Some days getting through to the other side is a perfectly acceptable goal. Every day can't be your best.
- Surviving my worst days has been a useful mantra. If it doesn't resonate with you, find your own. My sister-in-law uses Gary Allen's country song, *"Every Storm (Runs Out of Rain)"*.

3. TUNE OUT NEGATIVITY

Too often our ideas don't get the chance to grow because others point out all of the reasons they won't work. While this is often unintentional, it should be expected.

- Find people you trust and listen. Listen for ways to improve the idea, not ways to kill it.
- If everyone thought that your ideas are good ones, it likely would have been done already. This has been especially true in business.
- Schedule "worry time". Poke holes in ideas and work through all your doubts. Then, set them aside - it's time to create. My strategy has been to place skeptics in my inner circle to help highlight areas I might have glossed over and make my plans stronger. I'm not necessarily encouraging a "fire, ready, aim" approach, rather it's important to consciously address your worries and then move them out of the way.
- Be mindful about social media use. Do an assessment and make sure you are using it to serve you, not letting you serve it.

The pandemic and associated uncertainties in the economy are unsettling and for some downright cruel. For me, these uncertainties and the compounding events in my personal life left me with two options, I could accept defeat or find a new way forward. Everyday we can curl up in a ball and accept defeat or make the choice to focus on unfound opportunities, recognize that I'll survive my worst days, and tune out the negativity. I encourage you to pause and reflect on how this might help you navigate an uncertain future. There are opportunities, and plenty of room for growth. Let's all promise each other not to waste them!

14

Against All Average

— By Kyle Tolzman —

I had the best job in the world. I was well paid to represent SPARQ Training, Nike's new project in 2008 to get back into the cross-training scene. My team and I drove a lime green Isuzu box truck with superstars Adrian Peterson on one side, and Hope Solo on the other. We were packed to the roof with giveaways. Our team of three jumped from high school to high school countrywide to test the most talented athletes nationally. We were engaged in blogging, creating digital content, and uploading a variety of data about how each athlete performed. Coaches and players loved us for our crazy energy and fun-loving style. We were rock stars when we rolled into town. Each of us had a different strength but worked together to put on the best events possible. I was able to tap into my creativity, and we found our blog posts and videos were blowing up as the weeks went on. We had no idea what was going on outside our bubble, we felt like celebrities.

As we all know, the years between 2007 and 2009 were extremely rocky around the globe. These years were the biggest financial downturn since the Great Depression with people losing their jobs and homes left and right. We could see the pain, but we did not think that we would have to experience it. Initially untouched, we were naïve and living out our best lives. After returning home from our second tour of testing the top basketball programs in the Midwest, my co-workers and I were informed that the contract with Nike was not being renewed, and all of our trucks were placed in storage. Just like that, everything we had worked so hard to create, vanished. We were all jobless, I was devastated.

Life seemed fine at first. It was nice being at home and I found ample time to reconnect with some of my former high school classmates. I had a positive mindset, and was applying to new jobs every day, while sticking to a rigorous exercise schedule. I was lucky enough to be able to move back in with my parents and they welcomed me with open arms. As the weeks wore on I remember the extreme anxiety that set in as I went from job interview to job interview and was denied over and over again. I would check my phone up to 200 times a day to make sure that I didn't miss someone calling me about an opportunity. I had no rhythm or flow to my days. During that time, I spent 2-3 hours a day in the gym so that I wouldn't have the extreme stomach pains of raging anxiety brewing inside of me, with no hope for release. Each day, I awoke with a pounding heart, and feeling of sickness in my gut. I had so much pride in myself and my abilities that I believed I should have had a job offer already. Receiving unemployment felt mentally unacceptable and debilitating. It was tearing me apart that I was getting something for nothing.

As the weeks and months wore on with no solid, well-paying jobs in sight, I finally went into a temp agency to find work. As long as I was working it didn't matter what the job was, I had to start moving forward to put my mind at ease. I told myself that something was better than nothing at this point. Within days I was working for a cellular company processing credit cards payments from 4am-12pm for minimum wage. I went from a $40,000 a year job, using my creativity and energy, to making just a few dollars more than when I was on unemployment. I could pay for food and my student loans and that was about it. This was one of the lowest points of my life.

Baby Steps

When experiencing difficult times, it is extremely important to step back and look at the big picture. Although there will always be dark times in life, more often than not there is light at the end of the tunnel. I knew down deep in my heart that this was just a phase that I had to get through, and that everything happens for a reason. I transitioned into using a possibility mindset. I began to hold deep faith that if it was possible to be unemployed and depressed, on the other side of that, existed the possibility of living an extremely fulfilling life. What you think is possible can and will get you through tough times.

Although this time of my life was scary, I knew that action always outplays thought. I put one foot in front of the other and started the application process to get my Master's Degree in teaching. I did not focus on my current job, but instead shifted my focus to the future and put one foot in front of the other. This leap of faith completely changed the trajectory of my life, offering me a variety of skills and confidence that helped to propel my success both in the classroom, on the field, and during entrepreneurial ventures down the road. Once I finally said "yes" to the possibility of becoming a teacher and mentor to kids, the world started to work for me like it used to. Veteran teachers wanted to be my mentors and principals wanted me to student teach in their schools.

My parents continued to let me live rent free, nourished me with food, and allowed me to drive their vehicles. When we are down and out, we must not let fear or pity take the driver's seat. Making tough decisions towards positivity is needed during these times. Go forward, keep getting up, and let someone else have the pity party in your place. After all, you are against all average.

Fast Forward to 2020

As we all know life has its ups and downs and like many of you, 2020 hit me like a ton of bricks. As a high school educator, coach, entrepreneur, husband, and father, the Covid-19 pandemic has hit me from all angles. When the superintendent of our school district sent an email closing schools in March, my heart sank. I felt for the kids and all of the families whose worlds were about to get turned upside down. I wondered what my days were going to look like with all three of my kids at home from dawn to dusk. I wondered where students who relied on the school system for meals were going to get food. My head was spinning. I had prepared myself for this message, but I wasn't ready.

At the same time the school year was suspended, sports halted right along with it. All school district and city fields were closed, indefinitely. My main business in the sports world came to a screeching halt. No longer did kids in our community have a positive outlet to deal with the day-to-day emotions of growing up and being pent up. I had plans for a variety of programs for kids in grades K-12, but was forced to cancel them one by one. Governmental regulations and closed fields were my new reality. My busiest time of year became a time of emailing out disappointing news to families each week. Sadly, I am still sending them out as I write this on August 1st, 2020. It would be easy for me to find the negativity in this situation, but you've got to remember that I am against all average.

Becoming Against All Average

When you believe that the world is working for you and not against you, and you say yes to positive opportunities, beautiful things can happen. If I focused on the negative about not being able to run my company, I would never have been able to meet the Crazy Amazing™ people that I have over the past few months. Building skills and failing forward are essential components to getting through difficult times. Stop giving yourself so much time to think about how bad things are. Instead, be grateful and start giving without expectation. You've got this!

Against All Average has been a vision of mine for years. It has always pained me to see what happens to people when they think average is good enough. Growing up as an athlete, I wanted to be the best. I trained hard and tried to get as far away from average as possible. I didn't understand when teammates wouldn't try their absolute best in practice or games. The same philosophy kills me as a teacher and coach today. I see so much potential in kids and adults, but many have grown up to accept that being average is the stopping point. They can't see a bigger vision for themselves because they have been taught to fit certain molds and to stay in their comfort zones. This is why I created the Against All Average podcast.

The podcast is about giving people the skills and mindset to lead exceptional lives. To me, it doesn't matter if our listeners are entrepreneurs or not, the interviews and topics that we discuss are relevant and impactful to a wide range of circumstances. During this pandemic, launching the Against All Average podcast and building the brand has been just what I needed to get through this difficult time. I used what I had learned in 2009 and started putting one foot in front of the other and giving without expectation. I have met people I would have never thought possible, and was even introduced to Ann Marie Smith, who offered me a spot in this Crazy Amazing™ book. In difficult times you have to put yourself out there and just say yes. During this period of time I have been shaken to my core more times than I can count. However, just like I have always done in my life, I didn't allow fear to have a say in what I can or cannot accomplish. Fear is the extra energy I need to be great. If it's not scary, I don't do it. That is living an against all average life.

Against All Average Mindset

Possibility Mindset

When we fully think, understand, and believe that anything and everything is possible in our lives we will start living in a way that prepares us for success. If you don't think it can happen, it won't. If you think it is possible, it will.

Say Yes

Too often we overthink a positive opportunity. Keep it simple. If something is positive and moves you or your career forward, say yes to it. You never know what is on the other side of yes.

Be Grateful

You have to be grateful for where you are, and not where you are going. Every day on this earth is a blessing. Find positivity even in your darkest hours. Show and practice gratitude each and every day.

The World Works for You

You must understand that the only person in your way is you. The world works for us at all times. Difficult days are not setbacks, but simple lessons one must learn to move forward.

Giving Without Expectation

If you truly and wholeheartedly give without expectation or wanting recognition, you will be amazed at the fulfillment and success that comes back to you both emotionally and monetarily.

Fail Forward

Learn from your mistakes and continue to push forward. Those who fail forward the quickest reach the highest tiers of success.

Don't Pick and Choose Where You Put Your Energy

When things aren't going well in our lives we tend to pick and choose where we put our energy. Instead, maintain balance in your health, life, business, and relationships.

Be Solutions Based

Focus on a variety of solutions for each problem. Ask for help and ask for advice. Sometimes you need someone else's viewpoint to see the solution.

Sharpen Your Knife

When you are at your lowest, and feeling down and out, continue to work on yourself. Read a book, listen to a podcast, take a class online. With new skills comes confidence and new opportunity.

Action Outplays Thought

Small consistent action builds momentum. By taking action we can take our minds out of a consistent loop of anxiety, worry, and fear. Remember, a step in the wrong direction is better than no step at all. We learn from doing.

Bios

ANN MARIE SMITH

Ann Marie Smith is a keynote speaker, international best selling author and socially conscious serial entrepreneur. Ann Marie shares her personal journey of divorced, penniless and homeless to building an 8 figure net worth that today supports and creates opportunities for thousands. Ann Marie empowers and equips audiences to order and manifest a life where success meets significance. Over the years Ann Marie has been sought after as an expert by Forbes, Telemundo, Una Vision to name a few and has partnered with fellow thought leaders including: Jack Canfield, Robert Kiosaki and Tim Ballard on various business ventures.

Contact me at
216 S. Citrus #330,
West Covina, CA 91791

DR. BRITTANY FERNANDEZ

 Dr. Brittany Fernandez Wertz recently completed her residency in Family Medicine from Montclair Hospital Medical Center. During her time in residency, she held the position of chief resident and is currently building her own practice in Upland, California. She is a Los Angeles native and has a B.S. M.S. in Biology from UC San Diego. She obtained her degree as a Doctor of Osteopathic Medicine from Western University of Health Sciences, College of Osteopathic Medicine. Brittany enjoys visiting and laughing with family, running, and has recently started focusing her spare time compiling a series of children's books, The Adventures of Jack and Hudson. The purpose of the children's book series is to relate to today's youth and help ease adapting to various situations young children often encounter.

IRENE ABBOU

Irene is the creator of the Happiness Within Reach program which coaches high-achievers on how to create a more holistic approach to success. This teaches leaders evidence-based techniques to building more meaningful interpersonal connections while simultaneously growing their self-confidence and productivity. She is an ICF, ACC Certified life and business coach who holds two certifications from the University of Pennsylvania on Positive Psychology and is trained in the Gottman Method for Couples Therapy. Irene has helped hundreds of professionals get reacquainted with their hearts most affirming personal and professional desires and supports them to take action despite their fears. Her mission is to remind her clients of their indisputable worthiness and capability of creating an extraordinary life aligned with their highest truth.

IRIS POLIT

Iris Polit is a marketer, writer, speaker, and the founder of <u>Your Success Ace</u>. As a career and personal branding strategist, she is obsessed with human flourishing and believes that our work life plays a big role in our sense of fulfillment. Her mission is to help professionals and entrepreneurs get unstuck, take ownership of their success and live to their fullest potential. Iris leverages her training as an applied positive psychology practitioner, as well as two decades of experience in non-profit and corporate environments, to help her clients thrive through career transitions.

Embracing her multi-passionate nature, Iris is also a best-selling co-author of *Mastering the Art of Success* and co-producer of the 3-time Telly and 4-time Emmy Award-winning documentary, *A New Leash on Life: The K9s For Warriors Story*. Additionally, she recently joined a diverse and inclusive collective of female entrepreneurs and practitioners to launch *The*

Reboot, a virtual resource hub dedicated to educating and inspiring professional women who are looking to create transformation in their lives.

Iris currently resides in Austin and, in her spare time, enjoys travelling, live music, reading, hiking, and, most importantly, spending time and laughing with family and friends. If you would like to learn more about thriving through transitions, read her articles and visit: https://yoursuccessace.com/resources

JAIREK ROBBINS

#1 Bestselling Author Performance Coach & Lifestyle Entrepreneur Jairek Robbins is a man dedicated to helping professionals like you Achieve Success by Living With Purpose in your life and business.

At only 23 years old, Jairek was awarded the Congressional Award (Gold Medal) from the United States Congress.

He has conducted trainings for a variety of companies & organizations including... Harvard University, The United States Marines, The United States Air Force Special Forces, BMW, REMAX, UBS, Major League Baseball Teams and members of the U.S. Olympic team.

He is a trusted advisor and board member to a variety of different companies.

Today, the 34-year old with over a decade of performance coaching experience continues to unlock secrets for maximizing performance and organizational success (and he's just getting started).

JAKE SPERLEY

Jake Sperley is an entrepreneur, mentor, speaker, and advocate for young entrepreneurs. After starting multiple businesses at a young age, he has a unique perspective about learning from failure, facing adversity and continuing to pivot and grow new ventures.

In his current role as CEO of Fair and Event Marketplace & Software (www.fairandevent.com), he's committed to helping events use the latest in software and technology to help them flourish. The Pro Services division of his company specializes in website development, social media management, graphic design, and digital services to take any business to the next level.

Jake was raised in St.Helens Oregon on a small farm where he grew his love for entrepreneurship through a 4H program. He attended Oregon State University and graduated a year early with a B.S. in Business. He now resides in the Portland, Oregon area and in his spare time, enjoys being on the water, attending live events, eating epic food, and being with his family.

JESSE BRISENDINE

Jesse Brisendine, the creator of "Zero Limits Coaching," is a world renowned expert who works with individuals and organizations to move beyond their limitations & unlock their greatness.

Business leaders, Hollywood celebrities, entrepreneurs, medical professionals, and educators have utilized Jesse's services to break through limiting beliefs, uncover their unique purpose, build thriving businesses, and live fulfilling lives.

Jesse is a big fan of buffets, professional wrestling, and finding the silver lining in any situation.

JOCELYN KUHN

Jocelyn Kuhn is a professional coach, speaker and author with a wealth of experience helping people thrive through life's most challenging moments. She also works with many professionals in the industry, and working with them to create and market memorable experiences both on-line and live is one of her greatest passions.

As a coach and author she focuses her work on transitions — helping clients to clearly define new and exciting goals and dreams, reframe their story so that it empowers them, and create actionable steps towards achieving goals and overcoming obstacles. She's studied effective transitions at length and is excited to share her 5 Step process to thrive through any transitions a person may be facing in her first book Thriving Through Transitions.

Links:
Website: http://www.jocelynkuhn.com
Facebook: http://www.facebook.com/jocelynkuhn1
Instagram: http://www.instagram.com/jocelyn_kuhn

JOHN KRALIK (Superior Court Judge)

John Kralik is the author of A Simple Act of Gratitude (Hyperion 2011). He is a graduate of the University of Michigan Law School, and lives in Los Angeles where he serves as a judge. He is no longer on Facebook, but you can write him a letter at 2629 Foothill Blvd., No. 240, La Crescenta, CA 91214.

KYLE TOLZMAN

Kyle Tolzman is a teacher, entrepreneur, speaker, coach, podcaster, and writer. His experience over the past 17 years has helped him bring his message of action and excellence to thousands far and wide. His mission is to help as many people and organizations understand and believe that average mindset and actions lead to average lives and organizations. Tolzman is also the host of the Against All Average podcast where he interviews entrepreneurs and world changers about their lives, and key factors that have led them to where they are today. Be against all average!

If you would like to learn more about Kyle's latest project head to www.againstallaverage.com!

MICHELLE EADES

Michelle is an Oracle Card Intuitive and Explorer of Past Lives, located in Melbourne, Australia. After navigating life as an adult living with anxiety, she created the JOYFUL WARRIORS Card Deck, which contains 33 Strategies for Living An Authentic Life and a guidebook filled with wisdom and insights discovered along the way.

Her favorite saying is "You Are Amazing" and her favorite question to ask of New Friends is "Do You Know How AMAZING You Are?" What makes Michelle's heart sing, though, is finding the "Pieces of Me", all the stories and experiences that go to make her who she is now.

You are invited to connect with Michelle via www.michelleeades.com or email Michelle@joyexpress.com.au

MONICA GONZALES

Monica Gonzales A business-woman, entrepreneur, mom and wife. Monica is the co-founder of Aldabella Scarpa, Custom apparel and accessories for Children. Monica left the Dental Industry in 2008 to pursue her dream job of designing. Monica designed her first pair of children's shoes with a pair of scissors, double sided tape and a few crayons.

In 2012 Monica was named Entrepreneur of the Year by Verizon Wireless, 7th Annual Latina in Business of the Year and in 2013 California's Small Business of the Year recipient. Monica and her company have been featured around the world by broadcast outlets ABC, CBS, NBC, Telemundo, Univision, KCAL, along with printed Newpaper outlets. The heart and success of Monica's business has been Giving Back. To date thousands and thousands of our designer shoes have been donated across the USA to children in need. The love for design definitely came from Monica's Mom who began sewing at the age of 4. Monica grew up with parents that encourage her to purse her dreams and everyday supported the daily operations of Aldabella Scarpa.

Monica lives in Southern California with her husband, daughter and two dogs. January 2020 Monica passed her CA Realtors exam and is looking forward to exploring the Real

Estate market. She loves her daily routine of car dancing with the music blasting, getting a Starbucks with her daughter, lots of time with her family and friends. Monica is currently launching her own custom line of woman's accessories. Monica is a strong believer "if you choose a job you **LOVE** you will never have to work a day in your life."

If you would like to follow her and her daily fashion updates visit:

www.aldabellascarpa.com IG and FB @aldabellascarpa

TAMI HOLZMAN

Tami loves to make people happy – whether that means giving a confidence boost, an introduction to that person they just can't seem to get to, or strategic counseling on a not yet fully baked idea. She is passionate about helping people succeed.

Tami Holzman is the author of *From C-Student to the C-Suite*; in just three days from launch, *From C-Student to the C-Suite* became an Amazon bestseller and was ranked in the top 1% of sales on Amazon. From C-Student to the C-Suite is a modern-day guide to business and relationships – showing how a girl with straight C's in school but straight A's in Emotional Intelligence became savvy in the cutthroat business world.

Tami began her career in the entertainment industry as a talent agent, show creator and executive producer, with development deals at NBC, HBO, and the 20th Century Fox. During her time as an Executive Producer and creator of *Super Agent*, she discovered a white space for marketing to women through mainstream sports. The opportunity inspired Tami to co-found the Female Fan Group.

She segued into a successful career as the EVP of avVenta, a marketing services firm leading global business development, which led to a successful acquisition to Accenture. Shortly after, Tami served as a Chief Brand Officer of the Plastic Bank, a social impact company turning waste into currency.

Today, she is an LP and advisor with Halogen Ventures, corporate advisor, executive coach, and motivational speaker. Tami loves to mentor and promote opportunities for women.

Tami lives in Pacific Palisades, overlooking the Pacific Ocean where you can find her hosting friends while saluting the sun with a cocktail in hand and an ever-present smile on her face.

Tami is a guest lecturer at UCLA Marketing, USC, and Loyola Marymount Entrepreneurship courses.

In addition, Tami has a Certificate of Expertise from the University of Pennsylvania in Positive Psychology, with an emphasis on emotional intelligence, resilience skills, mental agility, and optimism.

WHITNIE WILEY

Whitnie Wiley is the founder and chief evolution officer (CEO) of Shifting Into Action (SIA), a coach, consultant, author, speaker and trainer.

As the premier next stage coach, Whitnie has over 25 years of experience coaching in the areas of dream and goal achieving, career management and transition, and leadership development. She helps new and aspiring leaders build and manage careers that feed their souls, use their talents and gifts, and finance the lives of their dreams through training programs and retreats, 1-on-1 and group coaching. Additionally, she provides consulting and coaching services to organizations relating to succession management, leadership development and training, human resources and talent development.

Prior to starting SIA, Whitnie was a lobbyist and the legal counsel for the Association of California Water Agencies, where she was responsible for creating and managing the legal department, as well as the association's legislative intern/externship and mentoring programs.

Whitnie's other leadership roles have included chair of the Association of Corporate Counsel's New-to-In House committee, service on the leadership development institute and the Docket advisory board. In addition, Whitnie was a member and served as chair of the California State Bar's Committee of Bar Examiners, a member of the leadership development institute for the California State Bar and chair of the Volunteer Center of Sacramento. She currently shares her expertise with nonprofit organizations through Catchafire and Lepris, and she can be heard frequently as a podcast guest.

For almost seven years, Whitnie authored the Lead the Way column for the Association of Corporate Counsel's Docket magazine, where she encouraged her readers to develop self-awareness and use their values and priorities to pave their path to enjoying their careers, better leadership and improved teamwork.

Whitnie is a contributing author to the bestselling book 1 Habit for Success and TAG Talks. Using her experience as a leader, along with observations and the feedback received from her readers and clients, Whitnie is looking forward to the publication of her forthcoming book "The SIMPLE Leader" and the official launch of The SIMPLE Leadership Method.

Whitnie holds a bachelor's degree in Organizational Behavior and Leadership from the University of San Francisco, a master's degree in Organizational Development and Leadership from St. Joseph's University and a juris doctor from Alliant International University's San Francisco Law School. She is a certified life coach with a specialty in career transitions and a Jack Canfield Certified Success Principles trainer.

She can be reached at: Whitnie@ShiftingIntoAction.com or 916.304.4742.

Additionally, you can find Whitnie on LinkedIn http://www.linkedin.com/in/whitniewiley and in her Facebook group www.facebook.com/groups/dreamjobcareerconnection.

LIST OF NON-PROFITS:

Arts for Kids - Whitnie Wiley
Anything Animal Related - Jesse Brisendine
Operation Underground Railroad

Made in the USA
Coppell, TX
08 October 2020